THE DISCOURSES OF EPICTETUS AND THE ENCHIRIDION

VOLUME ONE OF TWO

The Discourses of Epictetus
Epictetus c. 55 – 135 AD

Text set in 18 point Helvetica.
Chapter headings set in Helvetica Neue.

ISBN: 978-1-83412-389-9 Volume One
ISBN: 978-1-83412-390-5 Volume Two

THE DISCOURSES OF EPICTETUS AND THE ENCHIRIDION

VOLUME ONE OF TWO

EPICTETUS

GRAND TYPE CLASSICS

CONTENTS

VOLUME TWO

Book Three

Preface

ARRIANUS TO LUCIUS GELLIUS GREETING

I DID NOT WRITE down the Lectures of Epictetus in the form of a book, as one might do with such utterances as his, nor did I of my own will give them to the public, for, as I say, I did not write them down for publication. What I tried to do was to make notes of all that I used to hear him say word for word in the very language he used, so far as possible, and to preserve his sayings as reminders for myself hereafter of the nature of his mind and the directness of his speech. It follows then, as is natural, that the words are just such as a man might use to another on the impulse of the moment, not such as he would write for formal publication, with a view to a circle of readers hereafter. Moreover, such as they are, somehow or other they were put abroad among men without my consent and without my knowledge. Well, to me it is no great matter, if I appear in the world's eyes incapable of writing a book; and to Epictetus it will not matter in the least if men despise his lectures, for in the very act of giving them he made it plain that his one and only desire was to impel the minds of his hearers towards the noblest objects. If then these lectures should accomplish this result and no other, I take it they would be just what the lectures of philosophers ought to be; and if they fail, yet I would have those who read them understand that when Epictetus himself was speaking, his hearers were forced to feel just what he would have them feel. If the words read by themselves do not achieve this result, it may be that I am to blame, but it may be also that it could not be otherwise. Farewell.

BOOK ONE

CHAPTER ONE

On Things in our Power and Things not in our Power

OF OUR FACULTIES IN general you will find that none can take cognizance of itself; none therefore has the power to approve or disapprove its own action. Our grammatical faculty for instance: how far can that take cognizance? Only so far as to distinguish expression. Our musical faculty? Only so far as to distinguish tune. Does any one of these then take cognizance of itself? By no means. If you are writing to your friend, when you want to know what words to write grammar will tell you; but whether you should write to your friend or should not write grammar will not tell you. And in the same way music will tell you about tunes, but whether at this precise moment you should sing and play the lyre or should not sing nor play the lyre it will not tell you. What will tell you then? That faculty which takes cognizance of itself and of all things else. What is this? The reasoning faculty: for this alone of the faculties we have received is created to comprehend even its own nature; that is to say, what it is and what it can do, and with what precious qualities it has come to us, and to comprehend all other faculties as well. For what else is it that tells us that gold is a goodly thing? For the gold does not tell us. Clearly it is the faculty which can deal with our impressions. What else is it which distinguishes the faculties of music, grammar, and the rest, testing their uses and pointing out the due seasons for their use? It is reason and nothing else.

The gods then, as was but right, put in our hands the one blessing that is best of all and master of all, that and nothing else, the power to deal rightly with our impressions, but everything else they did not put in our hands. Was it that they would not? For my part I think that if they could have entrusted us with those other powers as well they would have done so, but they were quite unable. Prisoners on the earth and in an earthly body and among earthly companions, how was it possible that we should not be hindered from the attainment of these powers by these external fetters?

But what says Zeus? 'Epictetus, if it were possible I would have made your body and your possessions (those trifles that you prize) free and untrammelled. But as things are–never forget this–this body is not yours, it is but a clever mixture of clay. But since I could not make it free, I gave you a portion in our divinity, this faculty of impulse to act and not to act, of will to get and will to avoid, in a word the faculty which can turn impressions to right use. If you pay heed to this, and put your affairs in its keeping, you will never suffer let nor hindrance, you will not groan, you will blame no man, you will flatter none. What then? Does all this seem but little to you?'

Heaven forbid!

'Are you content then?'

So surely as I hope for the gods' favour.

But, as things are, though we have it in our power to pay heed to one thing and to devote ourselves to one, yet instead of this we prefer to pay heed to many things and to be bound fast to many–our body, our property, brother and friend, child and slave. Inasmuch then as we are bound fast to many things, we are burdened by them and dragged down. That is why, if the weather is bad for sailing, we sit distracted and keep looking continually and ask, 'What wind is blowing?' 'The north wind.' What have we to do with that? 'When will the west wind blow?' When it so chooses, good sir, or when Aeolus chooses. For God made Aeolus the master of the winds, not you. What follows? We must make the best of those things that are in our power, and take the rest as nature gives it. What do you mean by 'nature'? I mean, God's will.

'What? Am I to be beheaded now, and I alone?'

Why? Would you have had all beheaded, to give you consolation? Will you not stretch out your neck as Lateranus did in Rome when Nero ordered his beheadal? For he stretched out his neck and took the blow, and when the blow dealt him was too weak he shrank up a little and then stretched it out again. Nay more, on a previous occasion, when Nero's freedman Epaphroditus came to him and asked him the cause of his offence, he answered, 'If I want to say anything, I will say it to your master.'

What then must a man have ready to help him in such emergencies? Surely this: he must ask himself, 'What is mine, and what is not mine? What may I do, what may I not do?'

I must die. But must I die groaning? I must be imprisoned. But must I whine as well? I must suffer exile. Can any one then hinder me from going with a smile, and a good courage, and at peace?

'Tell the secret!'

I refuse to tell, for this is in my power.

'But I will chain you.'

What say you, fellow? Chain me? My leg you will chain–yes, but my will–no, not even Zeus can conquer that.

'I will imprison you.'

My bit of a body, you mean.

'I will behead you.'

Why? When did I ever tell you that I was

the only man in the world that could not be beheaded?

These are the thoughts that those who pursue philosophy should ponder, these are the lessons they should write down day by day, in these they should exercise themselves.

Thrasea used to say 'I had rather be killed to-day than exiled tomorrow'. What then did Rufus say to him? 'If you choose it as the harder, what is the meaning of your foolish choice? If as the easier, who has given you the easier? Will you not study to be content with what is given you?'

It was in this spirit that Agrippinus used to say–do you know what? 'I will not stand in my own way!' News was brought him, 'Your trial is on in the Senate!' 'Good luck to it, but the fifth hour is come'–this was the hour when he used to take his exercise and have a cold bath–'let us go and take exercise.' When he had taken his exercise they came and told him, 'You are condemned.' 'Exile or death?'

he asked. 'Exile.' 'And my property?' 'It is not confiscated.' 'Well then, let us go to Aricia and dine.'

Here you see the result of training as training should be, of the will to get and will to avoid, so disciplined that nothing can hinder or frustrate them. I must die, must I? If at once, then I am dying: if soon, I dine now, as it is time for dinner, and afterwards when the time comes I will die. And die how? As befits one who gives back what is not his own.

CHAPTER TWO

How One may be True to One's Character in Everything

TO THE RATIONAL CREATURE that which is against reason is alone past bearing; the rational he can always bear. Blows are not by nature intolerable.

'What do you mean?'

Let me explain; the Lacedaemonians bear flogging, because they have learnt that it is in accord with reason.

'But is it not intolerable to hang oneself?'

At any rate, when a man comes to feel that it is rational, he goes and hangs himself at once. In a word, if we look to it we shall see that by nothing is the rational creature so distressed as by the irrational, and again to nothing so much attracted as to the rational.

But rational and irrational mean different things to different persons, just as good and evil, expedient and inexpedient, are different for different persons. That is the chief reason why we need education, that we may learn so to adjust our preconceptions of rational and irrational to particular conditions as to be in harmony with nature. But to decide what is rational and irrational we not only estimate the value of things external, but each one of us considers what is in keeping with his character. For one man thinks it reasonable to perform the meanest office for another; for he looks merely to this, that if he refuses he will be beaten and get no food, while if he does it nothing hard or painful will be done to him. To another it seems intolerable not only to do this service himself, but even to suffer another to do it. If then you ask me, 'Am I to do it or not?' I shall say to you, to get food is worth more than to go without it, and to be flogged is worth less than to escape flogging: therefore, if you measure your affairs by this standard, go and do it.

'But I shall be false to myself.'

That is for you to bring into the question, not for me. For it is you who know yourself; you know at how much you put your worth, and at what price you sell yourself. For different men sell at different prices.

That is why Agrippinus, when Florus was considering whether he should go down to Nero's shows, to perform some part in them himself, said to him, 'Go down.' And when he asked, 'Why do you not go down yourself?' said, 'Because I do not even consider the question.' For when a man once lowers himself to think about such matters, and to value external things and calculate about them he has almost forgotten his own character. What is it you ask me? 'Is death or life to be preferred?' I say 'life'. 'Pain or pleasure?' I say 'pleasure'.

'But, if I do not act in the tragedy, I shall be beheaded.'

Go then and act your tragedy, but I will not do so. You ask me, 'Why?' I answer, 'Because you count yourself to be but an ordinary thread in the tunic.' What follows then? You ought to think how you can be like other men, just as one thread does not wish to have something special to distinguish it from the rest: but I want to be the purple, that touch of brilliance which gives distinction and beauty to the rest. Why then do you say to me, 'Make yourself like unto the many?' If I do that, I shall no longer be the purple.

Priscus Helvidius too saw this, and acted on it. When Vespasian sent to him not to come into the Senate he answered, 'You can forbid me to be a senator; but as long as I am a senator I must come in.'

'Come in then,' he says, 'and be silent.'

'Question me not and I will be silent.'

'But I am bound to question you.'

'And I am bound to say what seems right to me.'

'But, if you say it, I shall kill you.'

'When did I tell you, that I was immortal? You will do your part, and I mine. It is yours to kill, mine to die without quailing: yours to banish, mine to go into exile without groaning.'

What good, you ask, did Priscus do, being but one? What good does the purple do to the garment? Just this, that being purple it gives distinction and stands out as a fine example to the rest. Another man, had Caesar in such circumstances told him not to come into the Senate, would have said, 'Thank you for sparing me.' Such a one he would never have forbidden to come in; he would know that he would either sit silent like a pipkin or if he spoke would say what he knew Caesar wished and pile on more besides.

This spirit too was shown by a certain athlete, who was threatened with death if he did not sacrifice his virility. When his brother, who was a philosopher, came to him and said, 'Brother, what will you do? Are we to let the knife do its work and still go into the gymnasium?' he would not consent, but endured to meet his death. (**Here some one asked**, 'How did he do so, as an athlete or as a philosopher?') He did so as a man, and a man who had wrestled at Olympia and been proclaimed victor, one who had passed his days in such a place as that, not one who anoints himself at Bato's. Another man would have consented to have even his head cut off, if he could have lived without it.

That is what I mean by keeping your character: such is its power with those who have acquired the habit of carrying it into every question that arises.

'Go to, Epictetus, have yourself shaved.'

If I am a philosopher I say, 'I will not be shaved.'

'I must behead you then.'

Behead me, if it is better for you so.

One asked, 'How then shall we discover, each of us, what suits his character?'

How does the bull, he answered, at the lion's approach, alone discover what powers he is endowed with, when he stands forth to protect the whole herd? It is plain that with the possession of his power the consciousness of it also is given him. So each of us, who has power of this sort, will not be unaware of its possession. Like the bull, the man of noble nature does not become noble of a sudden; he must train through the winter, and make ready, and not lightly leap to meet things that concern him not.

Of one thing beware, O man; see what is the price at which you sell your will. If you do nothing else, do not sell your will cheap.

The great, heroic style, it may be, belongs to others, to Socrates and men like him.

'If then this is our true nature, why do not all men, or many, show it?'

What? Do all horses turn out swift, are all dogs good at the scent?

'What am I to do then? Since I have no natural gifts, am I to make no effort for that reason?'

Heaven forbid. Epictetus is not better than Socrates: if only he is as good as Socrates I am content. For I shall never be a Milo, yet I do not neglect my body; nor a Croesus, and yet I do not neglect my property; nor, in a word, do we abandon our effort in any field because we despair of the first place.

CHAPTER THREE

What Conclusions may be Drawn from the Fact that God is Father of Men

IF A MAN COULD only take to heart this judgement, as he ought, that we are all, before anything else, children of God and that God is the Father of gods and men, I think that he will never harbour a mean or ignoble thought about himself. Why, if Caesar adopts you, your arrogance will be past all bearing; but if you realize that you are a son of Zeus, will you feel no elation? We ought to be proud, but we are not; as there are these two elements mingled in our birth, the body which we share with the animals, and the reason and mind which we share with the gods, men in general decline upon that wretched and dead kinship with the beasts, and but few claim that which is divine and blessed.

And so, since every one, whoever he be, must needs deal with each person or thing according to the opinion that he holds about them, those few who think that they have been born to be faithful, born to be honourable, born to deal with their impressions without error, have no mean or ignoble thought about themselves. But the thoughts of most men are just the opposite to this. 'What am I? A miserable creature of a man'; and 'my wretched rags of flesh'. Wretched indeed, but you have too something better than your 'rags of flesh'. Why then do you discard the better and cling to your rags?

By reason of this lower kinship some of us fall away and become like wolves, faithless and treacherous and mischievous, others like lions, savage and brutal and untameable, but the greater part of us become foxes and the most god-forsaken creatures in the animal world. For a foul-mouthed and wicked man is no better than a fox or the meanest and most miserable of creatures. Look to it then and beware lest you turn out to be one of these god-forsaken creatures.

CHAPTER FOUR

On Progress, or Moral Advance

HOW SHALL WE DESCRIBE 'progress'? It is the state of him who having learnt from philosophers that man wills to get what is good, and wills to avoid what is evil, and having learnt also that peace and calm come to a man only if he fail not to get what he wills, and if he fall not into that which he avoids, has put away from him altogether the will to get anything and has postponed it to the future, and wills to avoid only such things as are dependent on his will. For if he tries to avoid anything beyond his will, he knows that, for all his avoidance, he will one day come to grief and be unhappy. And if this is the promise that virtue makes to us–the promise to produce happiness and peace and calm, surely progress toward virtue is progress toward each of these. For to whatever end the perfection of a thing leads, to that end is progress an approach.

How is it then that, though we admit that this is the nature of virtue, we search elsewhere for progress and display it elsewhere?

What does virtue produce?

Peace of mind.

Who then makes progress? Is it he who has read many treatises of Chrysippus? Can this be virtue–to have understood Chrysippus? For if this be so, we must admit that progress is nothing but to understand a lot of sayings of Chrysippus. But, the fact is, we admit that virtue tends to one result, and yet declare that progress, the approach to virtue, tends to another.

'Yonder man', he says, 'can already read Chrysippus by himself.'

Bravo, by the gods, you make progress, fellow. Progress indeed! Why do you mock him? Why do you draw him away from the sense of his own shortcomings? Will you not show him what virtue really means, that he may learn where to seek for progress? Miserable man, there is only one place to seek it–where your work lies. Where does it lie? It lies in the region of will; that you may not fail to get what you will to get, nor fall into what you will to avoid; it lies in avoiding error in the region of impulse, impulse to act and impulse not to act: it lies in assent and the withholding of assent, that in these you may never be deceived. But the first department I have named comes first and is most necessary. If you merely tremble and mourn and seek to escape misfortune, progress is of course impossible.

Show me your progress then in this field. You act as though when I was talking to an athlete and said, 'Show me your shoulders', he answered, 'Look at my leaping-weights.' That is for you and your leaping-weights to look to; I want to see the final result of your leaping-weights.

'Take the treatise on "Impulse" and learn how I have read it.'

Slave, that is not what I am looking for–I want to know what impulses you have, for action and against it, to know what you will to get and will to avoid; how you plan and purpose and prepare–whether in harmony with nature, or out of harmony with nature. Show me that you act in harmony with nature, and I will tell you that you are making progress; act out of harmony with nature, and I bid you begone and write books on such things and not merely expound them. What good, I ask, will they do you? Do not you know that the whole book is worth but five pence? Do you think then that the man who expounds it is worth more? Therefore never seek your work in one place and progress in another.

Where then is progress?

If any one of you, dismissing things without, has brought his mind to bear on his own will, to work out its full development, that he may bring it into perfect harmony with nature–lofty, free, unhindered, untrammelled, trustworthy, self-respecting; if he has learnt that he that wills to get or to avoid what is not in his power cannot be trustworthy nor free, but must needs himself change as they change, fitful as the winds, and must needs have made himself subservient to others, who can procure or hinder such things; and if, in a word, when he rises in the morning he guards and keeps these principles, washes as one that is trustworthy, eats as one that is self-respecting, and on each occasion that arises labours to achieve his main tasks, even as the runner makes running his one aim and the voice-trainer his training–he is the man who is indeed in the path of progress and who has not travelled to no purpose.

But if all his efforts are turned to the study of books, if on this he spends his labour, and for this has gone abroad, then I bid him go straight home and not neglect what he finds there; for this that he has gone abroad for is nothing; his true work is to study to remove from his life mourning and lamentation, the 'ah me' and 'alas for my misery', the talk of 'bad fortune' and 'misfortune'; and to learn, what is death, what is exile, what is imprisonment, what is the cup of hemlock; that he may be able to say in prison, 'My dear Crito, if it pleases the gods, so be it', and not such words as 'miserable old man that I am, is it for this I kept my grey hairs?' (Plato, **Crito**, 43d) Whose words are they? Do you think I shall name to you a mean man of no reputation? Are they not the words of Priam and of Oedipus? Are they not the words of all kings that are? For what else are tragedies but a portrayal in such metrical form of the sufferings of men who have set their admiration on outward things? If delusion after all were the only means for a man to learn this lesson–the lesson that not one of the things beyond the compass of our will concerns us, then I for my part would choose a delusion such as this, if it should procure me a life of undisturbed tranquillity; I leave it to you to see what you choose.

What then does Chrysippus offer us?

'That you may know', he says, 'that these truths from which tranquillity and peace of mind come to men are not false–take my books and you shall find that what gives me peace of mind is true and in harmony with nature.'

O great good fortune! O great benefactor, who shows us the way! And yet–though all men have raised temples and altars to Triptolemus, for teaching us the cultivation of the crops, yet what man of you ever set up an altar in honour of him who found the truth and brought it to light and published it among all men–not the truth of mere living, but the truth that leads to right living? Who ever dedicated a shrine or an image for this gift, or worships God for it? I say shall we, who offer sacrifices because the gods gave us wheat or the vine, never give thanks to God that they produced this manner of fruit in the mind of men, whereby they were to show us the true way of happiness?

CHAPTER FIVE

Against Followers of the Academy

IF A MAN, says Epictetus, objects to what is manifestly clear, it is not easy to find an argument against him, whereby one shall change his mind. And this is not because of his power, nor because of the weakness of him that is instructing him; but, when a man, worsted in argument, becomes hardened like a stone, how can one reason with him any more?

Now there are two ways in which a man may be thus hardened: one when his reasoning faculty is petrified, and the other when his moral sense is petrified, and he sets himself deliberately not to assent to manifest arguments, and not to abandon what conflicts with them. Now most of us fear the deadening of the body and would take all possible means to avoid such a calamity, yet we take no heed of the deadening of the mind and the spirit. When the mind itself is in such a state that a man can follow nothing and understand nothing, we do indeed think that he is in a bad condition; yet, if a man's sense of shame and self-respect is deadened, we even go so far as to call him 'a strong man'.

Do you comprehend that you are awake?

'No,' he says, 'no more than I comprehend it, when I seem to be awake in my dreams.'

Is there no difference then between the one sort of impression and the other?

'None.'

Can I argue with him any longer? What fire or sword, I say, am I to bring to bear on him, to prove that his mind is deadened? He has sensation and pretends that he has not; he is worse than the dead. One man does not see the battle; he is ill off. This other sees it but stirs not, nor advances; his state is still more wretched. His sense of shame and self-respect is cut out of him, and his reasoning faculty, though not cut away, is brutalized. Am I to call this 'strength'? Heaven forbid, unless I call it 'strength' in those who sin against nature, that makes them do and say in public whatever occurs to their fancy.

CHAPTER SIX

On Providence

EACH SINGLE THING THAT comes into being in the universe affords a ready ground for praising Providence, if one possesses these two qualities–a power to see clearly the circumstances of each, and the spirit of gratitude therewith. Without these, one man will fail to see the usefulness of nature's products and another though he see it will not give thanks for them. If God had created colours and, in general, all visible things, but had not created a faculty to behold them, of what use would they be? None at all. If on the other hand He had created this faculty, but had not created objects of such a nature as to fall under the faculty of vision, even so of what use would it be? None at all. If again He had created both these, and had not created light, even so there would be no use in them. Who is it then that has adapted this to that, and that to this? Who is it that has fitted the sword to the scabbard and the scabbard to the sword? Is there no one? Surely the very structure of such finished products leads us commonly to infer that they must be the work of some craftsman, and are not constructed at random. Are we to say then that each of these products points to the craftsman, but that things visible and vision and light do not? Do not male and female and the desire of union and the power to use the organs adapted for it–do not these point to the craftsman? But if these things are so, then the fact that the intellect is so framed that we are not merely the passive subjects of sensations, but select and subtract from them and add to them, and by this means construct particular objects, nay more, that we pass from them to others which are not in mere juxtaposition–I say are not these facts sufficient to rouse men's attention and to deter them from leaving out the craftsman? If it be not so, let them explain to us what it is which makes each of these things, or how it is possible that objects so marvellously designed should have come into being by chance and at random?

Again, are these faculties found in us alone? Many in us alone–faculties which the rational creature had special need of–but many you will find that we share with irrational creatures. Do they also then understand events and things? No–for using is one thing, and understanding is another. God had need of them as creatures dealing with impressions, and of us as dealing with them and understanding them as well. That is why it is enough for them to eat and drink and rest and breed, and every function is theirs which each irrational creature fulfils; while we, to whom He gave also the power of understanding, cannot be satisfied with these functions, but, unless we act with method and order and consistently with our respective natures and constitutions, we shall no longer attain to our end. For those whose constitutions are different have also different functions and different ends. Therefore that which by constitution is capable only of using things, is satisfied to use them anyhow; but that which by constitution is capable of understanding things as well as using them, will never attain its end, unless to use it adds method also. What is my conclusion? God makes one animal for eating, and another for service in farming, another to produce cheese, and others for different uses of a like nature, for which there is no need of understanding impressions and being able to distinguish them; but He brought man into the world to take cognizance of Himself and His works, and not only to take cognizance but also to interpret them. Therefore it is beneath man's dignity to begin and to end where the irrational creatures do: he must rather begin where they do and end where nature has ended in forming us; and nature ends in contemplation and understanding and a way of life in harmony with nature. See to it then that ye do not die without taking cognizance of these things.

You travel to Olympia, that you may see the work of Phidias, and each of you thinks it a misfortune to die without visiting these sights, and will you have no desire to behold and to comprehend those things for which there is no need of travel, in the presence of which you stand here and now, each one of you? Will you not realize then who you are and to what end you are born and what that is which you have received the power to see?

'Yes, but there are unpleasant and hard things in life.'

Are there none such at Olympia? Are you not scorched with heat? Are you not cramped for room? Is not washing difficult? Are you not wet through when it is wet? Do you not get your fill of noise and clamour and other annoyances? Yet I fancy that when you set against all these hardships the magnificence of the spectacle you bear them and put up with them. And have you not received faculties, which will enable you to bear all that happens to you? Have you not received greatness of spirit? Have you not received courage? Have you not received endurance? If I am of a great spirit what concern have I in what may happen? What shall shake me or confound me or seem painful to me? Instead of using my faculty for the purpose for which I have received it, am I to mourn and lament at the events of fortune?

'Yes, but my rheum flows.'

Slave! What have you hands for then? Is it not to wipe your rheum away?

'Is it reasonable then that there should be rheum in the world?'

Well, how much better it is to wipe your rheum away than to complain! What do you think would have become of Heracles if there had not been a lion, as in the story, and a hydra and a stag and a boar and unjust and brutal men, whom he drove forth and cleansed the world of them? What would he have done, if there had been nothing of this sort? Is it not plain that he would have wrapped himself up and slept? Nay to begin with he would never have been a Heracles at all, had he slumbered all this life in such ease and luxury; and if by any chance he had been, of what good would he have been? What use would he have made of his arms and his might and his endurance and noble heart as well, had not he been stimulated and trained by such perils and opportunities?

'Was it his duty then to contrive these occasions for himself and to seek means to bring a lion, a boar, or a hydra into his country?'

That were madness and folly; but as they had come into being and were found in the world these monsters were of service to display Heracles' powers and to train them.

It is for you then, when you realize this, to look to the faculties you possess, and considering them to say, 'Zeus, send me what trial Thou wilt; for I have endowments and resources, given me by Thee, to bring myself honour through what befalls.' Nay, instead, you sit trembling for fear of what may happen, or lamenting, mourning, and groaning for what does happen, and then you reproach the gods. What else but impiety indeed can attend upon so ignoble a spirit as yours? And yet God not only gave us these faculties, which will enable us to bear all the issue of events without being humiliated or broken down by it, but, as became a good king and a true father, He gave us this gift free from all let or hindrance or compulsion–nay, He put it wholly in our hands, not even leaving Himself any power to let or hinder us. Yet possessing thesepowers in freedom for your own you refuse to use them and will not realize what gifts you have received and from whose hand, but you sit mourning and grieving, some of you blinded to the giver Himself and refusing to recognize your benefactor, and some from meanness of spirit turning to reproaches and complaints against God. Yet I will show you that you have resources and endowment to fit you for a noble and courageous spirit: show me, if you can, what endowments you have for complaining and reproach.

CHAPTER SEVEN

On the Use of Variable Premisses and Hypothetical Arguments and the Like

MOST MEN IGNORE THE fact that the treatment of variable premisses and hypothetical arguments and again of syllogisms that conclude by way of question, and, in a word, of all such arguments is concerned with conduct. For really, whatever subject we are dealing with, our aim is to find how the good man may fitly deal with it and fitly behave towards it. It follows then that either they must say that the virtuous man will not condescend to question and answer, or that if he does he will take no care to avoid behaving lightly and at random in questioning and answering; or else, if they accept neither alternative, they must admit that we have to investigate those subjects round which question and answer chiefly turn. For what do we promise in a discussion? To establish what is true, to remove what is false, to withhold assent in what is uncertain. Is it enough then merely to learn that this is so?

'It is enough.'

Is it enough then for him who wishes not to go wrong in the use of coin merely to be told why you accept genuine drachmas and reject spurious ones?

'It is not enough.'

What then must you acquire besides? Surely you must have a faculty to test and distinguish genuine drachmas from spurious. Is it not true . then in regard to argument also that merely to hear what is said is not enough; a man must acquire the faculty to test and distinguish the true from the false and the uncertain?

'It must be so.'

This being so, what is required in argument?

'Accept what follows from the premisses you have duly granted.'

Here again, is it enough merely to know this? No, you must learn how a conclusion follows from the premisses, and how sometimes one proposition follows from one other, and sometimes from many together. May we say then that this faculty too must be acquired by him who is to behave with good sense in discussion, and who is himself to prove each point in his demonstration and to follow the demonstrations of others, and to avoid being led astray by sophistical arguments, posing as demonstrations? Thus it comes about that we are led to think it really necessary to discuss and to practise the arguments and moods which are conclusive.

But note this: there are cases where we have granted the premisses properly, and such and such a conclusion follows which, though it follows, is none the less false. What then is it fitting for me to do? Must I accept the false conclusion? How can I do that? Must I say I was wrong in granting the premisses?

'No, you may not do this either.'

That it does not follow from the premisses granted?

'No, you may not do this.'

What then is one to do in these circumstances? May we not say that just as in order to be in debt it is not enough merely to borrow, but one must remain a borrower and not have paid off the loan, so in order to be bound to admit an inference it is not enough to have granted the premisses, but one must abide by having granted them?

In a word, if they remain to the end as we granted them, we are absolutely bound to remain by our concessions and accept what follows the premisses; if, on the other hand, they do not remain as they were granted, we are also absolutely bound to abandon the concession and no longer to accept what is inconsistent with the premisses; for since we have abandoned our agreement as to the premisses, this inference which is drawn no longer concerns us or touches us. We must then examine into premisses of this sort and into such changes and alterations in them, by which they are changed in the actual process of question or answer or syllogism or the like, and so afford occasion to the foolish to be troubled because they do not see the sequence of the argument. Why must we do so? That in this sphere we may do what is fitting by avoiding what is random or confused in argument.

And we ought to do the same with hypotheses and hypothetical arguments. For it is necessary sometimes to assume a hypothesis as a step to the next argument. Must we then concede every given hypothesis or not? And if not every one, which? And, having conceded it, must we abide by it once for all and maintain it, or are we sometimes to abandon it, and are we to accept what follows from it and reject what conflicts with it?

'Yes.'

But a man says, 'If you accept a hypothesis of what is possible, I will reduce you in argument to what is impossible.'

Will the prudent man refuse to meet him in argument, and avoid examination and discussion with him? Nay, it is just the prudent man who is capable of reasoning logically and who is expert at questioning and answering, yes and who is proof against deception and sophistry. Will he then consent to argue, but take no pains to avoid being careless and casual in argument? If so, will he not cease to be the man we consider him to be? But without some such training and preparation as I suggest can he guard the sequence of his argument? Let them show that he can, and then all these speculations are idle; they were absurd and inconsistent with the conception we have formed of the good man.

Why do we persist in being lazy and indolent and sluggish, why do we seek excuses to enable us to avoid toiling early and late to perfect ourselves in logical theory?

'Do you call it parricide if I go wrong in logic?'

Slave, here is no father for you to kill. You ask what you have done, you have committed the one error which was possible in this field. Your answer is the very one I made myself to Rufus when he rebuked me because I could not find the one missing step in a syllogism. 'Well,' said I, 'I suppose I have not burnt the Capitol down'; and he answered, 'Slave, the missing step here is the Capitol.'

You are not going to tell me, are you, that setting fire to the Capitol and killing one's father are the only forms of wrongdoing? To deal with one's impressions without thought or method, to fail to follow argument or demonstration or sophism, in a word, to be unable to see what concerns himself and what does not in question and answer–is there no wrongdoing, I ask, in any of these?

CHAPTER EIGHT

That Faculties are Fraught with Danger for the Uneducated

JUST AS IT IS possible to interchange terms which are equivalent to one another, so and in just as many ways it is allowable to vary in argument the types of disputative argument and enthymeme. Take for instance this kind of argument: 'If you borrowed and did not repay, you owe me the money. You did not borrow without repaying; therefore you do not owe me the money.' And the philosopher above all others is the proper person to handle such arguments with skill. For if enthymeme is imperfect syllogism, plainly he who is trained in perfect syllogism would be equally capable in dealing with imperfect.

Why then, you ask, do we not train ourselves and one another in this style of argument? Because even now, though we do not devote ourselves to training in these matters and though we are not drawn away, so far as I have any influence, from cultivating character, nevertheless we make no advance towards goodness. What should we have to expect then, if we should add this business to our other employments? And there is more–not only should we have less leisure for more necessary things, but we should give uncommon occasion for conceit and vanity. For the faculty of disputative and plausible reasoning is a powerful one, especially if it should be developed by training and gain further dignity from mastery of language. For indeed generally every faculty is dangerous when it comes into the hands of those who are without education and without real force, for it tends to exalt and puff them up. For how would it be possible to persuade the young man who excels in these arguments that he ought not to become dependent upon them, but to make them depend upon him? Instead of this he tramples under foot all we say to him and walks among us in a high state of elation, so puffed up that he cannot bear that any one should remind him how far he has fallen short and into what errors he has lapsed.

'What do you mean? Was not Plato a philosopher?'

I reply, Was not Hippocrates a physician? But you see how eloquent Hippocrates was. Was Hippocrates so eloquent by virtue of being a physician? Why then do you mix qualities, which are casually united in the same persons? Suppose Plato was handsome and strong; ought I also to set to and strive to become handsome or strong, as though this were necessary for philosophy, just because one philosopher was handsome as well? Will you not have the discernment to see what makes men philosophers and what qualities are accidental in them? Suppose now I were a philosopher, ought you to become lame?

You ask me, do I then count these faculties as of no effect?

Heaven forbid! no more than I ignore the faculty of vision. Nevertheless if you ask me what is the true good of man, I can only say to you that it lies in a certain disposition of the will.

CHAPTER NINE

How One may Draw Conclusions from the Fact that we are God's Kinsmen

IF THESE STATEMENTS OF the philosophers are true, that God and men are akin, there is but one course open to men, to do as Socrates did: never to reply to one who asks his country, 'I am an Athenian', or 'I am a Corinthian', but 'I am a citizen of the universe.' For why do you say that you are an Athenian, instead of merely a native of the little spot on which your bit of a body was cast forth at birth? Plainly you call yourself Athenian or Corinthian after that more sovereign region which includes not only the very spot where you were born, and all your household, but also generally that region from which the race of your forbears has come down to you. When a man therefore has learnt to understand the government of the universe and has realized that there is nothing so great or sovereign or all-inclusive as this frame of things wherein men and God are united, and that from it come the seeds from which are sprung not only my own father or grandfather, but all things that are begotten and that grow upon earth, and rational creatures in particular – for these alone are by nature fitted to share in the society of God, being connected with Him by the bond of reason–why should he not call himself a citizen of the universe and a son of God? Why should he fear anything that can happen to him among men? When kinship with Caesar or any other of those who are powerful in Rome is sufficient to make men live in security, above all scorn and free from every fear, shall not the fact that we have God as maker and father and kinsman relieve us from pains and fears?

'And where am I to find food to eat, if I have nothing?' says one.

Well, what do slaves do when they leave their masters, or what do they rely on? Do they rely on fields, or servants, or silver plate? No, on nothing but themselves; nevertheless sustenance does not fail them. And shall our philosopher in his wanderings have to rest his confidence in others, instead of taking care of himself? Is he to be baser and more cowardly than the unreasoning beasts? For each one of them is content with itself, and lacks not its proper sustenance nor the way of life that is naturally suited to it.

I think that the old man who sits here to teach you ought to devote his skill not to save you from being low-minded, and from reasoning about yourselves in a low and ignoble spirit, but rather to prevent young men from arising of the type who, discovering their kinship with the gods, and seeing that we have these fetters attached to us in the shape of the body and its possessions and all that we find necessary for the course and management of our life by reason of the body, may desire to fling all these away as vexatious and useless burdens and so depart to the gods their kindred.

And so your teacher and instructor, if he were a true teacher, should engage in this conflict of argument:

You come saying, 'Epictetus, we can bear no longer to be bound with the fetters of this wretched body, giving it meat and drink and rest and purgation, and by reason of the body having to adapt ourselves to this or that set of circumstances. Are not these things indifferent and as nothing to us, and death no evil thing? Are we not kinsmen of the gods, from whom we have come hither? Suffer us to depart to the place whence we have come, suffer us to be released from these bonds that are fastened to us and weigh us down. Here are robbers and thieves and law-courts and so-called kings, who by reason of our poor body and its possessions are accounted to have authority over us. Suffer us to show them that they have authority over nothing.'

Hereupon I answer: 'Men as you are, wait upon God. When He gives the signal and releases you from this service, then you shall depart to Him; but for the present be content to dwell in this country wherein He appointed you to dwell. Short indeed is the time of your dwelling here, and easy for them whose spirit is thus disposed. What manner of tyrant or what thief or what law-courts have any fears for those who have thus set at nought the body and its possessions? Stay where you are, and depart not without reason.' Such should be the answer of the teacher to his gifted pupils. How different is what we see! There is no life in your master, and no life in you. When you have had your fill to-day, you sit groaning about the morrow, and how you are to find food. Slave, if you get food, you will have it; if not, you will depart: the door is open. Why do you whine? What room is there for tears any more? What occasion for flattery any more? Why should one envy another? Why should he gaze with wonder on them that are rich or powerful, especially if they be strong and quick to anger? For what will they do with us? We will pay no heed to what they have power to do, what we really care for they cannot touch. Who, I ask you, will be master over one who is of this spirit?

How did Socrates approach these matters? Surely as one should who is convinced of his kinship with the gods. 'If you tell me,' he says, '"We; acquit you on condition that you discourse no longer as you have done hitherto, and that you do not annoy young or old among us"', I shall answer, 'It is absurd for you to suppose that, while I am bound to maintain and guard any post to which your general appointed me, and should rather die ten thousand times than abandon it, yet if God has appointed us to a certain place and way of life we ought to abandon that.' [Plato, **Apology**, 29c, 28e] Here you see a man who is a kinsman of the gods in very truth. But as for us–we think of ourselves as if we were all belly and flesh and animal desire; such are our fears, such our passions; those that can help us to these ends we flatter, and at the same time fear.

Some one has asked me to write for him to Rome, one who, as the world thought, had had misfortunes; he had once been famous and rich, and had now lost everything and was living here. So I wrote for him in a humble tone. And he read my letter and gave it me back and said, ‘I wanted your help, not your pity.’ So, too, Rufus, to try me, used to say, ‘Your master will do this or that to you’; and when I answered him, ‘This is the lot of man’, ‘Why then’, said he, ‘do I appeal to your master when I can get everything from you?’ for, indeed, it is true that what a man has of himself it is idle and futile for him to receive from another. Am I then, who can get from myself the gift of a noble and lofty spirit, to get from you a field or money or office? Heaven forbid! I will not be so blind to my true possessions. But when a man is mean and cowardly, for him one must needs write letters as for one that is dead. ‘Make us a present of the corpse of so and so and his miserable quart of blood.’ For indeed such a one is a mere corpse and a quart of blood and nothing more. If he were anything more, he would have realized that one man cannot make another miserable.

CHAPTER TEN

To those who nave Spent their Energies on Advancement in Rome

IF WE HAD BEEN as earnest and serious about our work as old men in Rome are about their concerns, we too might perhaps have achieved something. I know what was said to me by a man older than myself who is now in charge of the corn-supply in Rome, when he passed through here on his way back from exile; he ran down his former life and made great professions for the future, saying that when once he was back he would have no other interest except to live out the rest of his life in peace and tranquillity, 'For how little I have still left me', said he.

And I said to him, 'You will not do it; so soon as you sniff the air of Rome you will forget all your professions'; and I told him that if he got a chance of entering the Palace, he would thrust his way in and give God thanks.

'Epictetus,' he answered, 'if you find me putting one foot in the Palace, believe what you like of me.'

Well, what did he do? Before he came to Rome, a dispatch from the Emperor met him, and as soon as he got it he forgot all he had said and has gone on adding to his heap ever since. I should like to stand by him now and remind him of the words he used as he passed through, and say to him, 'How much more clever a prophet am I than you!'

What conclusion do I draw? Do I say that the creature man is not to be active? Heaven forbid! But what is it that fetters our faculty of action? Take myself first: when day comes, I remind myself a little as to what lesson I ought to read to my pupils. Then in a moment I find myself saying, 'But what do I really care what sort of lesson I give to this man or that? The first thing is for me to sleep.' And yet how can their business be compared in importance with ours? If you attend to what they are doing you will see the difference. They do nothing all day long except vote, dispute, deliberate about a handful of corn or an acre of land, and petty profits of this sort. Is there any resemblance between receiving and reading a petition such as this: 'I beg you to let me export a little corn', and a petition such as, 'I beg you to inquire from Chrysippus how the universe is governed and what position the rational creature holds in it; inquire too who you are and what is good for you, and what is evil'? What have these petitions in common? Do both demand the same attention? Is it equally shameful to neglect one and to neglect the other?

What is my conclusion? Are we elders alone indolent and sleepy? Nay, the fault is much rather with you young men. For indeed, we old folk, when we see young men playing, are only too eager and ready to join their play. Much more, if I saw them thoroughly awakened and eager to share my studies, should I be eager myself to take my studies seriously too.

CHAPTER ELEVEN

On Family Affection

WHEN AN OFFICIAL CAME to Epictetus and inquired for special directions he asked whether he had a wife and children; and when the man said, 'Yes', he asked again, How do you get on?

'Miserably', he said.

What do you mean? said he; Men do not marry and have children to the end that they may be miserable, but rather that they may be happy.

'Ah', said he, 'but I am so miserable about my poor children, that lately when my daughter was ill and was thought to be in danger I could not bear to be near her, but fled away from her, until some one brought me news that she was well.'

Well, do you think you were right to do it?

'It was natural', he said.

Nay, said the master, only convince me that it was natural, and I will convince you that everything that is natural is right.

'All fathers', he said, 'or most of us, at least, feel like that.'

I do not deny, said Epictetus, that parents feel so, but the real question is whether it is right. No doubt as far as that goes, we must say that even tumours come into being for the good of the body, and in a word that error is natural, for nearly all, or most of us at least, are prone to error. Prove to me then how it is natural.

'I cannot'; he said, 'rather do you prove to

me how it is wrong or unnatural.'

He answered, Suppose we were discussing black and white, what test should we call in to distinguish between them?

'The sight', he said.

What if we were discussing things hot or cold, hard and soft, what test should we use?

'Touch.'

Well then, as we are discussing what is natural and right and the opposite, what test would you have us take?

'I do not know', said he.

Look here, it is no great loss perhaps not to know the proper test for colours and smells, nay, and flavours too, but do you think it is a small loss to man not to know what is good and what is evil, what is natural and what is unnatural?

'No, the greatest possible loss.'

Tell me now, is everything right which seems noble and fitting to certain people? To-day, for instance, are the opinions of

Jews and Syrians, Egyptians and Romans, as to food all of them right?

'How can they be?'

No, I suppose if the Egyptians' views are right the other nations' must of necessity be wrong; if the Jews' opinions are good, other people's must be bad.

'Of course.'

And where there is ignorance, there is also want of insight and education as to necessary things.

'Yes.'

When once you have realized this, then, said Epictetus, you will make this your one interest in the future, and to this alone devote your mind–to discover the means of judging what is natural and to use your criterion to distinguish each particular case as it arises.

For the present I can help you just so far as this in regard to what you wish: do you think family affection is natural and good?

'Of course.'

Again, is it true that affection is natural

and good, and reason not good?

'Certainly not.'

Is there a conflict then between reason and affection?

'I think not.'

If there were a conflict, then, as one of the two is natural, the other must needs be unnatural?

'Certainly', he said.

It follows then that whenever we find reason and affection united in an action, we confidently affirm that it is right and good.

'Granted', he said.

Mark what follows. I do not think you will deny that it is not reasonable to leave one's child when it is ill and to go away. The only question left for us is to consider whether it is affectionate.

'Let us consider it then.'

Was it right, I ask, for you, being affectionately disposed to your child, to run away and leave her? Is her mother not fond of the child?

'She is indeed.'

Should the mother then have left her too, or should she not?

'She should not.'

What of the nurse? Is she fond of the child?

'She is', he said.

Ought she then to have left her?

'By no means.'

Again, is not the child's attendant fond of her?

'He is.'

Ought he then to have gone away and left her? Was it right that as a consequence the child should be thus left desolate and helpless because of the great affection of you its parents and of those about it, or should die in the hands of those who had no love or care for it?

'Heaven forbid!'

Once more, it is not fair or reasonable, is it, that a man should not allow others equally affectionate with himself to do what, because he is affectionate, he thinks proper for himself. It is absurd. Tell me, would you have liked, if you were ill, your relations and every one else, even your wife and children, to show their affection for you in such a way as to leave you alone and desolate?

'Certainly not.'

Would you pray to be so loved by your own people, as to be always left alone by them when you were ill, because of their exceeding affection, or would you, if it were a question of being left alone, rather pray, supposing that were possible, to have the affection of your enemies? And if that is so, we are forced to the conclusion that your conduct was not that of affection.

What reason had you then? Was there nothing which moved and impelled you to abandon the child? How is that possible? It must have been the same sort of motive, which once made a man in Rome cover his eyes when the horse he had backed was running, and then again when the horse unexpectedly won made him faint so that he needed sponges to recover him. What is the motive? This perhaps is not the moment to define it; but it is enough that we should be convinced of this –if what philosophers say is sound–that we must not look for it somewhere outside us, but that it is always one and the same motive which causes us to do or not to do a thing, to speak or not to speak, to be elated or depressed, to fly or to pursue–the very motive which has moved you and me at this moment, you to come and sit and listen to me, and me to say what I do. What is the motive? Surely it is nothing but this–that we are so minded?

'Nothing else.'

And if things had looked different to us, we should still have done what we were minded to do and nothing else. So when Achilles mourned, his reason was, not the death of Patroclus–for another man, when his comrade dies, is not thus affected–but that he was so minded. So in your case, you ran away just because you were so minded; and again, if you stay it will be because you are so minded. And now you return to Rome, because you have a mind to do so; and if your mind changes, you will not depart thither. And in a word it is not death nor exile nor pain nor any such thing which is the cause of our action or inaction, but thoughts and judgements of the mind. Are you convinced of this or not?

'I am', he said.

Then on each occasion the effects of an action correspond to the causes. So henceforward whenever we do a thing wrong, we shall blame nothing else but the judgement which led us to do it, and we shall try to remove and extirpate this even more than we do tumours and abscesses from the body. And so also we shall assert that our right actions are determined in the same way; and we shall no longer blame neighbour or wife or children as though they caused evils to befall us, being convinced that, unless we make up our mind that things are such, we' do not act as though they were, but that whether we judge them to be so or not depends upon ourselves and not on anything outside us.

'True', he said.

From this day forward then we shall not investigate or examine the nature or condition of anything else–whether it be land or slaves or horses or dogs–but only our own judgements.

'I hope so', said he.

You see then that you must become a student–that creature whom all mock at–if you really wish to investigate your judgements. That this is not the work of an hour or a day you fully understand without my telling you.

CHAPTER TWELVE

On Contentment

CONCERNING THE GODS THERE are some who say that the Divine does not exist, others that it exists but is inactive and indifferent and takes no thought for anything, others again that God does exist and take thought but only for great things and things in the heavens, but for nothing on earth; and a fourth class say that God takes thought also for earthly and human things, but only in a general way, and has no care for individuals: and there is a fifth class, to whom belong Odysseus and Socrates, who say

> **where'er I move**
> **Thou seest me**.
>
> [Homer, Iliad, X. 279]

Before all things then it is necessary to examine each of these views, to see whether it is true or untrue. For if there are no gods, how can following the gods be the end of man? If again there are gods, but they care for nothing, in that case too what good will it be to follow them? But once more, if they exist and do care, yet if there is no communication between them and men, nay what is more, if there is none between them and me, to follow them cannot be a true end. The good man then, having examined into all these questions, has submitted his mind to Him that orders the universe, as good citizens submit to the law of the city. The man who is under education ought to approach education with this purpose in his mind: 'How can I follow the gods in everything, and how can I be content with the divine governance and how can I become free?' For he is free, for whom all things happen according to his will and whom no one can hinder.

'What then? Is freedom the same as madness?'

Heaven forbid! frenzy and freedom have nothing in common.

'But', you say, 'I want everything to happen as I think good, whatever that may be.'

Then you are in a state of madness, you are out of your mind. Do you not know that freedom is a noble thing, and worthy of regard? But merely to want one's chance thoughts to be realized, is not a noble thing; it comes perilously near being the most shameful of all things. How do we act in matters of grammar? Do I want to write Dion's name as I will? No, I am taught to will the right way of writing. How is it in music? Just the same. So it is universally, in every region of art or science. Otherwise it would not be worth while to know anything, if everything conformed itself to each man's will.

Are we to say then that in this sphere alone, the greatest and most momentous of all, the sphere of freedom, it is permitted me to indulge chance desires? By no means: education is just this–learning to frame one's will in accord with events. How do events happen? They happen as the Disposer of events has ordained them. He ordained summer and winter, fruitful and barren seasons, virtue and vice and all such opposites for the sake of the harmony of the universe, and gave to each one of us a body and bodily parts and property and men to associate with.

Remembering then that things are thus ordained we ought to approach education, not that we may change the conditions of life, that is not given to us, nor is it good for us–but that, our circumstances being as they are and as nature makes them, we may conform our mind to events.

I ask you, is it possible to avoid men? How can we? Can we change their nature by our society? Who gives us that power? What is left for us then, or what means do we discover to deal with them? We must so act as to leave them to do as seems good to them, while we remain in accord with nature.

But you are impatient and discontented; if you are alone you call it a wilderness, and if you are with men you describe them as plotters and robbers, and you find fault even with your own parents and children and brothers and neighbours.

Why, when you are alone you ought to call it peace and freedom and consider yourself the equal of the gods; when you are in a large company you should not call it a crowd or a mob or a nuisance, but a high-day and a festival, and so accept all things in a spirit of content.

What punishment is there, you ask, for those who do not accept things in this spirit? Their punishment is to be as they are. Is one discontented with being alone? Let him be deserted. Is one discontented with his parents? Let him be a bad son, and mourn his lot. Is one discontented with his children? Let him be a bad father.

'Cast him into prison.'

What do you mean by prison? he is in prison already; for a man's prison is the place that he is in against his will, just as, conversely, Socrates was not in prison, for he chose to be there.

'Am I then to have a maimed leg?'

Slave, do you mean to arraign the universe for one wretched leg? Will you not make a gift of it to the sum of things? Will you not resign it? Will you not joyfully yield it up to Him who gave it? Will you be vexed and discontented with the ordinances of Zeus, laid down and ordained by Him witl- the Fates who were present at your birth and span your thread of life? Do you not know, what a little part you are, compared with the universe? I say this of your body, for in reason you are not inferior to the gods nor less than they; for the greatness of reason is judged not by length or height but by its judgements.

Will you not then set your good in that region where you are equal to the gods?

'Alas, but look what a father and mother I have got!'

Why? was it given you on entering life to choose and say, 'Let such an one marry such an one at this hour, that I may be born?' No such choice was given you: your parents had to be in existence first, and your birth had to follow. Of what parents? Of such as they were.

Well then, as your parents are what they are, is no resource left you? Surely if you did not know to what end you possess the faculty of vision, you would be unhappy and miserable if you closed your eyes, when colours were brought near you; but are you not more wretched and unhappy still for not knowing that you have a high and noble spirit to face each occasion as it arises? The objects which correspond to the faculty that you have are brought near you: yet you turn away your faculty just at the very moment when you ought to keep it open-eyed and alert. Rather give thanks to the gods that they set you above those things which they put out of your power, and made you responsible only for what is within your control. For your parents they left you without responsibility; and the same is true of brothers, body, property, death, life. For what then did they make you responsible? For that which alone is in your power, the proper handling of your impressions. Why then do you insist on dragging in these things for which you are not responsible? That is to make trouble for yourself.

CHAPTER THIRTEEN

How One may Act in All Things so as to Please the Gods

WHEN SOME ONE ASKED Epictetus how one may eat so as to please the gods, he said, If you can eat justly, and with good feeling and, it may be, with self-control and modesty, may you not also eat so as to please the gods? And when you call for hot water and the slave does not answer, or answers and brings it luke-warm, or is not to be found in the house, is it not pleasing to the gods that you should not be angry nor break into a passion?

'How then is one to bear with such persons?'

Slave, will you not bear with your own brother, who has Zeus for his forefather, and is born as a son of the same seed as you and of the same heavenly descent? You were appointed to a place of superiority like this, and are you straightway going to constitute yourself a despot? Will you not remember what you are and whom you are ruling? that they are kinsmen, born your brothers, children of Zeus?

'But I have bought them, and they have not bought me.'

Do you see where your eyes are looking? You are looking at the earth, at what is lowest and basest, at these miserable laws of the dead, and you regard not the laws of the gods.

CHAPTER FOURTEEN

That God Beholds All Men

WHEN ONE ASKED HIM how a man may be convinced that every one of his acts is seen by God, Do you not think, he said, that all things are united together?

'I do', he said.

Again, do you think that things on earth feel the influence of things in heaven?

'I do', he said.

Whence comes it that in such perfect order

as at God's command, when He bids the plants to flower, they flower, when He bids them grow, they grow, when He bids them to bear fruit, they bear, when to ripen, they ripen; when again He bids them drop their fruit, they drop it, and when to let fall their leaves, they let them fall, and when He bids them gather themselves up and be still and take their rest, they are still and take their rest? Whence is it that as the moon waxes and wanes and as the sun draws near and departs afar we behold so great a change and transformation of things on the earth? If the plants then and our own bodies are so closely bound up with the universe, and so share its affections, is it not much more so with our minds? And if our minds are so bound up with God and in such close touch with Him as being part and portion of His very being, does not God perceive their every movement as closely akin to Him?

Consider this: you, a man, have power to reflect on the divine governance and on each divine operation as well as upon things human, you have the faculty of being moved in your senses and your intelligence by countless objects, sometimes assenting, sometimes rejecting, sometimes doubting; you guard in your own mind these many impressions derived from so many and various objects, and moved by them you conceive thoughts corresponding to those objects which have first impressed you, and so from countless objects you derive and maintain one after another the products of art and memory.

All this you do, and is God not able to behold all things and be present with all and to have some communication with all? Why, the sun is able to illuminate so large a part of the universe, and to leave unilluminated only so much as the shadow which the earth makes can cover: and cannot He who has created the sun itself, and who makes it to revolve–a small part of Himself as compared with the whole–has not He, I say, the power to perceive all things?

'But', says one, 'I cannot comprehend all these things at once.'

Of course no one tells you that in faculty you are equal to Zeus. Nevertheless He has set by each man his genius o guard him, and committed each man to his genius to watch over, ay and a genius which sleeps not and is not to be beguiled. To what other guardian, better or more attentive, could He have committed each one of us? Therefore, when you close your doors and make darkness within, remember never to say that you are alone: you are not alone, God is within, and your genius. What need have they of light to see what you are doing? To this God you ought to swear allegiance from the first as the soldiers swear to Caesar. They are paid servants, yet they swear that they will put the safety of Caesar above all things: and shall you not swear too, who have been counted worthy of so many and so great blessings, or having sworn shall you not keep your oath? And what shall your oath be? Never to disobey, never to accuse, never to find fault with any of God's gifts, never to let your will rebel, when you have to do or to bear what necessity demands. Can the soldier's oath be compared with ours? The soldiers swear to respect no man above Caesar, but we to respect ourselves first of all.

CHAPTER FIFTEEN

What Philosophy Professes

WHEN A MAN CONSULTED Epictetus how to persuade his brother to be angry with him no longer, he replied, 'Philosophy does not promise to secure to man anything outside him. If it did it would be admitting something beyond its subject-matter. For as wood is the material dealt with by the carpenter, bronze by the statuary, so the subject-matter of each man's art of living is his own life. What are we to say then of your brother's life? That again is the concern of his art of living: to yours it is a thing external, like land, health, good repute. Philosophy makes no promises about such things.'

'In all circumstances' (says philosophy), 'I will keep the Governing Principle in accord with nature.'

Whose Governing Principle?

'His, in whom I am.'

How then am I to prevent my brother from being angry with me? Bring him to me and I will tell him, but I have nothing to say to you about his anger.

When the man who consulted him said, 'What I am looking for is this–how I may be in accord with nature, even though he be not reconciled with me', he replied, No great thing comes suddenly into being, any more than a cluster of grapes or a fig. If you say to me now, 'I want a fig', I shall answer that it needs time. Let it flower first, then put forth its fruit and then ripen. I say then, if the fig tree's fruit is not brought to perfection suddenly in a single hour, would you gather fruit of men's minds so soon and so easily? I tell you, you must not expect it.

CHAPTER SIXTEEN

On Providence

MARVEL NOT THAT THE other creatures have their bodily needs supplied–not only meat and drink, but a bed to lie on–and that they want no shoes nor rugs nor clothes, while we want all these things. For it would not have been a good thing that these creatures, born not for themselves but for service, should have been created liable to wants. Consider what it would be for us to have to take thought not only for ourselves but for sheep and asses, how they were to dress and what shoes they were to put on, and how they should find meat and drink. But just as soldiers when they appear before their general are ready shod, and clothed and armed, and it would be a strange thing indeed if the tribune had to go round and shoe or clothe his regiment, so also nature has made the creatures that are born for service ready and prepared and able to dispense with any attention. So one small child can drive sheep with a rod.

Yet we forbear to give thanks that we have not to pay the same attention to them as to ourselves, and proceed to complain against God on our own account. I declare, by Zeus and all the gods, one single fact of nature would suffice to make him that is reverent and grateful realize the providence of God: no great matter, I mean; take the mere fact that milk is produced from grass and cheese from milk and wool from skin. Who is it that has created or contrived these things?

'No one', he says.

Oh, the depth of man's stupidity and shamelessness!

Come, let us leave the chief works of nature, and behold what she works by the way. Is anything more useless than the hairs upon the chin? Did she not use even these in the most suitable way she could? Did she not by these means distinguish male and female? Does not the nature of each one of us cry aloud from afar, 'I am a man: on these terms approach me and address me; seek nothing else. Behold the signs.' Again, in women nature took the hair from their face, even as she mingled in their voice a softer note. What! You say the creature ought to have been left undistinguished and each of us to have proclaimed, 'I am a man'? Nay, but how noble and comely and dignified is this sign, how much more fair than the cock's crest, how much more magnificent than the lion's mane! Therefore we ought to preserve the signs God has given; we ought not to abandon them, nor, so far as in us lies, to confound the sexes which have been distinguished.

Are these the only works of Providence in us? Nay, what words are enough to praise them or bring them home to us? If we had sense we ought to do nothing else, in public and in private, than praise and bless God and pay Him due thanks. Ought we not, as we dig and plough and eat, to sing the hymn to God? 'Great is God that He gave us these instruments wherewith we shall till the earth. Great is God that He has given us hands, and power to swallow, and a belly, and the power to grow without knowing it, and to draw our breath in sleep.' At every moment we ought to sing these praises and above all the greatest and divinest praise, that God gave us the faculty to comprehend these gifts and to use the way of reason.

More than that: since most of you are walking in blindness, should there not be some one to discharge this duty and sing praises to God for all? What else can a lame old man as I am do but chant the praise of God? If, indeed, I were a nightingale I should sing as a nightingale, if a swan, as a swan: but as I am a rational creature I must praise God. This is my task, and I do it: and I will not abandon this duty, so long as it is given me; and I invite you all to join in this same song.

CHAPTER SEVENTEEN

That the Processes of Logic are Necessary

SINCE IT IS REASON which makes all other things articulate and complete, and reason itself must be analysed and made articulate, what is it that shall effect this? Plainly, reason itself or something else. That something else either is reason or it will be something superior to reason, which is impossible. If it is reason, who again will analyse that reason? For if it analyses itself, so can the reason with which we started. If we are going to call in something else, the process will be endless and unceasing.

'Yes,' says one, 'but the more pressing need is not logic but the discipline of men's thoughts and feelings', and the like.

If you want to hear about moral improvement, well and good. But if you say to me, 'I do not know whether you argue truly or falsely', and if I use an ambiguous word and you say to me 'distinguish', I shall grow impatient and say to you, 'this is the more pressing need.' It is for this reason, I suppose, that men put the processes of logic in the forefront, just as we put the testing of the measure before the measuring of the corn. And if we do not determine first what is the bushel and what is the scale, how shall we be able to measure or weigh anything? So in the sphere of thought if we have not fully grasped and trained to perfection the instrument by which we judge other things and understand other things, shall we ever be able to arrive at accurate knowledge? Of course, it is impossible.

'Yes,' they say, 'but the bushel is a mere thing of wood and bears no fruit.'

True, but it can measure corn.

'The processes of logic, too, are unfruitful.'

This we will consider presently: but even if one should concede this, it is enough that logic has the power to analyse and distinguish other things and in fact, as one might say, has the power to weigh and measure. Who asserts this? Is it only Chrysippus and Zeno and Cleanthes? Does not Antisthenes agree? Why, who is it that has written, 'The beginning of education is the analysis of terms'? Does not Socrates too say the same? Does not Xenophon write of him that he began with the analysis of terms, to discover what each means?

Is this then what you call great and admirable–to understand or interpret

Chrysippus? Nay, no one says that. What is admirable then? To understand the will of Nature. Very well: do you understand it of yourself? If so, what more do you need? For if it is true that all error is involuntary and you have learnt the truth, you must needs do rightly hereafter.

'But,' you may say, 'I do not understand the will of Nature.'

Who then expounds it? They say 'Chrysippus.' I come and inquire what this interpreter of Nature says. I begin not to understand what he means and I seek some one to interpret. The interpreter says, 'Let us examine the sense of this phrase, as if it were Latin.'

Why, pray, should the interpreter put on airs? Even Chrysippus has no right to do so, if he is only expounding the will of Nature, and does not follow it himself: how much less his interpreter. For we have no need of Chrysippus for his own sake, but only to enable us to follow Nature: just as we have no need, for himself, of the priest who offers sacrifice, but because we think that through him we shall understand the signs which the gods give of the future, nor do we need the sacrifice for itself, but because through it the sign is given, nor do we marvel at the crow or the raven but at God who gives His signs by them.

So I come to this interpreter and priest and say, 'Examine the victim's flesh to see what sign is given me.' He takes and opens the flesh and interprets, 'Man, you have a will unhindered and unconstrained by nature. This is written here in the flesh of the sacrifice. I will show you the truth of it first in the sphere of assent. Can any one prevent you from agreeing to what is true? No one. Can any one compel you to accept the false? No one. Do you see that in this sphere your faculty is free from let and hindrance and constraint and compulsion? Is it any different in the sphere of will and impulse? What, I ask, can overcome impulse except another impulse? And what can overcome the will to get or will to avoid except another will to get or to avoid?'

'If he threatens me with death,' one says, 'he compels me.'

No, it is not what he threatens you with which compels you, but your decision that it is better to do what you are bidden than to die. Once more then it is your own judgement which compels you–that is, will puts pressure on will. For if God had so created that portion of His own being which He has taken from Himself and given to us, that it could suffer hindrance or compulsion from another, He would cease to be God and to care for us as He must needs do. 'This', says the priest, 'is what I find in the sacrifice: this is God's sign to you: if you will, you are free: if you will, you will blame no one, you will accuse no one: everything shall be in accordance with your own mind and the mind of God.'

This is the prophecy which draws me to consult this seer and philosopher, and his interpretation makes me admire not him but the truths which he interprets.

CHAPTER EIGHTEEN

That we should not be Angry at Men's Errors

IF WHAT PHILOSOPHERS SAY is true, that in all men action starts from one source, feeling, as in assent it is the feeling that a thing is so, and in denial the feeling that it is not so, yes, by Zeus, and in withholding judgement, the feeling that it is uncertain: so also impulse towards a thing is originated by the feeling that it is fitting, and will to get a thing by the feeling that it is expedient for one, and it is impossible to judge one thing expedient and will to get another, and to judge one thing fitting and be impelled to another. If all this be true, why are we angry with the multitude?

'They are thieves', he says, 'and robbers.'

What do you mean by thieves and robbers?

'They are gone astray and know not what is good and what is evil.'

Ought we then to be angry with them or to pity them? Only show them their error and you will see how they desist from their faults. But if their eyes are not opened, they regard nothing as superior to their own judgement.

'What!' you say. 'Ought not this robber and this adulterer to be put to death?'

Nay, say not so, but rather, 'Should I not destroy this man who is in error and delusion about the greatest matters and is blinded not merely in the vision which distinguishes white and black, but in the judgement which distinguishes good and evil?' If you put it this way, you will recognize how inhuman your words are; that it is like saying, 'Should I not kill this blind man, or this deaf one?' For if the greatest harm that can befall one is the loss of what is greatest, and a right will is the greatest thing in every one, is it not enough for him to lose this, without incurring your anger besides? Man, if you must needs harbour unnatural feelings at the misfortune of another, pity him rather than hate him; give up this spirit of offence and hatred: do not use these phrases which the backbiting multitude use, 'These accursed and pestilent fools'.

Very well. How are you suddenly converted to wisdom? What an angry temper you show!

Why then are we angry? Because we admire the material things of which they rob us. For only cease to admire your clothes, and you are not angry with him who steals them: cease to admire your wife's beauty, and you cease to be angry with the adulterer. Know that the thief and adulterer have no place among things that are your own, but only among things that are another's and beyond your power. If you let them alone and count them as nothing you have no one to be angry with any more. But as long as you admire these things you must be angry with yourself rather than with them. For, look you, you have fine clothes, your neighbour has none: you have a window, you wish to air them. He does not know what is the true good of man, but fancies, as you do too, that it is to have fine clothes. Is he not to come then and carry them off? Why, if you show a cake to greedy men, and gobble it down all to yourself, do you expect them not to snatch at it? Do not provoke them, do not have a window, do not air your clothes.

For my part, yesterday I had an iron lamp beside my household gods, and hearing a noise I rushed to the window. I found the lamp had been carried off. I reasoned with myself, that the man who took it yielded to some plausible feeling. What do I conclude? To-morrow, I say, you will find one of earthenware. The truth is, a man loses only what he has. 'I have lost my cloak.' Yes, for you had one. 'I have got a headache.' Have you a horn-ache too? Why then are you vexed? Your losses and your pains are concerned only with what you possess.

'But the tyrant will chain me.'

Yes, your leg.

'But he will cut off.'

What? Your neck. But what will he fail to bind or cut off? Your will. That is why the men of old enjoined 'Know thyself.' What follows? You ought to practise in small things and go on from them to greater.

'I have a headache.'

Then do not say, 'Ah me!'

'I have earache.'

Do not say, 'Ah me!' And I do not mean that you may not groan, but do not groan in spirit. And if the boy brings you your leg-bands slowly, do not cry out loud and pull a long face and say, 'Every one hates me.' Who is not likely to hate such an one?

Put confidence in these thoughts for the future and walk erect and free, not relying on bulk of body like an athlete. For you do not need to be invincible by brute force like an ass.

Who then is the man who is invincible? He whom nothing beyond his will can dismay. So I go on observing him in each set of circumstances as if he were an athlete. He has overcome the first round. What will he do in the second? What if it be a hot sun, and the struggle is in Olympia?

So it is in life. If you offer a man a trifle of silver, he will scorn it. What will happen if you offer him a young. maid? What if you do it in the dark? What happens if you ply him with reputation, or abuse, or praise, or death? All these he can conquer. What will he do if he is wrestling in the hot sun, I mean, if he has drunk too much? What if he is in a frenzy, or in sleep? The man who can overcome in all these circumstances is what I mean by the invincible athlete.

CHAPTER NINETEEN

How One should behave towards Tyrants

IF A MAN POSSESSES some advantage, or thinks he does though he does not, he is bound, if he be uneducated, to be puffed up because of it. The tyrant, for instance, says, 'I am mightiest of all men.'

Well, and what can you give me? Can you enable me to get what I will to get? How can you? Can you avoid what you will to avoid, independent of circumstances? Is your impulse free from error? How can you claim any such power?

Tell me, on shipboard, do you put confidence in yourself or in the man who knows? And in a chariot? Surely in him who knows. How is it in other arts? Exactly the same. What does your power come to then?

'All men pay me attention.'

Yes, and I pay attention to my platter and work it and polish it and I fix up a peg for my oil-flask. Does that mean that these are superior to me? No, but they do me some service, and for this reason I pay them attention. Again: do I not pay attention to my ass? Do I not wash his feet? Do I not curry him? Do you not know that every man pays regard to himself, and to you only as to his ass? For who pays regard to you as a man? Show me. Who wishes to become like you? Who regards you as one like Socrates to admire and follow?

'But I can behead you.'

Well said. I forgot, of course, one ought to pay you worship as if you were fever or cholera, and raise an altar to you, like the altar to Fever in Rome.

What is it then which disturbs and confounds the multitude? Is it the tyrant and his guards? Nay, God forbid! It is impossible for that which is free by nature to be disturbed or hindered by anything but itself. It is a man's own judgements which disturb him. For when the tyrant says to a man, 'I will chain your leg,' he that values his leg says, 'Nay, have mercy,' but he that values his will says, 'If it seems more profitable to you, chain it.'

'Do you pay no heed?'

No, I pay no heed.

'I will show you that I am master.'

How can you? Zeus gave me my freedom. Or do you think that he was likely to let his own son be enslaved? You are master of my dead body, take it.

'Do you mean that when you approach me, you pay no respect to me?' No, I only pay respect to myself: if you wish me to say that I pay respect to you too, I tell you that I do so, but only as I pay respect to my water-pot.

This is not mere self-love: for it is natural to man, as to other creatures, to do everything for his own sake; for even the sun does everything for its own sake, and in a word so does Zeus himself. But when he would be called 'The Rain-giver' and 'Fruit-giver' and 'Father of men and gods', you see that he cannot win these names or do these works unless he does some good to the world at large: and in general he has so created the nature of the rational animal, that he can attain nothing good for himself, unless he contributes some service to the community. So it turns out that to do everything for his own sake is not unsocial. For what do you expect? Do you expect a man to hold aloof from himself and his own interest? No: we cannot ignore the one principle of action which governs all things–to be at unity with themselves.

What follows? When men's minds harbour wrong opinions on things beyond the will, counting them good and evil, they are bound to pay regard to tyrants. Would that it were only tyrants, and not chamberlains too! How can a man possibly grow wise of a sudden, when Caesar appoints him to the charge of the privy? How is it we straightway say, 'Felicio has spoken wisely to me'? I would fain have him deposed from the dung-heap, that he may seem foolish to you again. Epaphroditus had a shoemaker, whom he sold because he was useless: then by some chance he was bought by one of Caesar's officials, and became Caesar's shoemaker. If you could have seen how Epaphroditus honoured him. 'How is my good Felicio, I pray you?' Then if some one asked us, 'What is your master doing?' the answer was, 'He is consulting Felicio about something.' What, had he not sold him for useless? Who has suddenly made a wise man of him? This is what comes of honouring anything outside one's will.

He has been honoured with a tribuneship. All who meet him congratulate him; one kisses his eyes, another his neck, his slaves kiss his hands. He comes into his house and finds lamps being lighted. He goes up to the Capitol and offers sacrifice. Who, I ask you, ever offered sacrifice in gratitude for right direction of the will or for impulse in accordance with nature? For we give thanks to the gods for what we think our good!

To-day one spoke to me about the priesthood of Augustus. I told him, 'Fellow, leave the thing alone; you will spend a great deal on nothing.'

'Well, but those who draw up contracts will record my name.'

Can you be there when men read it and say to them, 'That is my name,' and even supposing you can be there now, what will you do if you die?

'My name will remain.'

Write it on a stone and it will remain. But who will remember you outside Nicopolis?

'But I shall wear a golden crown.'

If you desire a crown at all, take a crown of roses and wear that: you will look smarter in that.

CHAPTER TWENTY

How Reason has the Faculty of Taking Cognizance of Itself

EVERY ART AND FACULTY has certain principal things of which it is to take cognizance. When therefore the faculty itself is of like kind with the objects of which it takes cognizance, it must of necessity have power to take cognizance of itself: when it is of unlike kind, it cannot take cognizance of itself. For instance, the shoemaker's art is concerned with hides, but itself is absolutely different from the material of hides: for this reason it does not take cognizance of itself. Grammar again is concerned with written speech: is it then written speech itself? Certainly not: therefore it cannot take cognizance of itself.

For what purpose then have we received reason from nature? That we may deal with impressions aright.

What then is reason itself?

A system framed from impressions of a certain kind. Thus it naturally has the power to take cognizance of itself.

Again, sagacity has been given us. To take cognizance of what? Things good and bad and indifferent.

What is it then itself?

Good.

And what is folly?

Bad. Do you see then that of necessity sagacity has the power of taking cognizance of itself and its opposite? Therefore the primary and highest task of the philosopher is to test impressions and distinguish them and to make use of none which is untested. Consider how we have invented an art to test the currency, in which we are admitted to have some interest. Look how many means the assayer uses to test the coin –sight, touch, smell, finally hearing: he breaks the penny and attends to the sound, and is not content with hearing its note once, but by much attention gets an ear for music.

Thus, where we think it makes a serious difference to us whether we are right or wrong, we take great pains to distinguish the possible sources of error, and yet when we have to do with our Governing Principle itself, poor thing, we gape and sleep and are ready to accept any impression that comes: for we do not notice our loss.

When you wish, therefore, to realize how little concerned you are about good and evil, and how eager about things indifferent, consider how you regard physical blindness on the one hand, and mental delusion on the other, and you will recognize that you are far from having a proper feeling in regard to things good and evil.

'Yes, but it needs much preparation and much toil and study.'

What of that? Do you expect that a brief study will enable you to acquire the greatest art? Yet the principal doctrine of philosophers itself is brief enough. If you will learn it, read Zeno's words and you will see. For it is no long matter to say man's end is to follow the gods, and the essence of good is the power of dealing rightly with impressions.

'Tell us then what is "God," and what is "impression," and what is nature in the individual, and what in the universe'.

That is a long story.

Again, if Epicurus should come and say, that the good must be in the flesh, that too means a long discussion; it means we must be taught what is the commanding faculty in us, what constitutes our substantial and true nature. If it is not probable that the good of the snail is in the shell, is it probable that man's good is in his body? Take yourself, Epicurus. What is the more masterful faculty you possess? What is it in you which deliberates, which examines everything, which examines the flesh itself and decides that it is the principal thing? Why do you light a lamp and toil for us, and write such big volumes? Is it that we may not be ignorant of the truth? Who are we? What concern have we with you? So the argument becomes a long one.

CHAPTER TWENTY ONE

To those who Wish to be Admired

WHEN A MAN HAS his proper station in life, he does not hanker after what is beyond him.

What is it, man, that you wish to have?

'I am content if I am in accord with Nature in what I will to get and will to avoid, if I follow Nature in impulse to act and to refrain from action, in purpose, and design and assent.'

Why then do you walk about as if you had swallowed a poker?

'I would fain that they who meet me should admire me, and cry aloud, "What a great philosopher!"'

Who are these by whom you wish to be admired? Are not these the men whom you generally describe as mad? What do you want then? Do you want to be admired by madmen?

CHAPTER TWENTY TWO

On Primary Conceptions

PRIMARY CONCEPTIONS ARE common to all men, and one does not conflict with another. Who among us, for instance, does not assume that the good is expedient and desirable and that we ought in all circumstances to follow and pursue it? Which of us does not assume that the just is noble and becoming?

At what moment then does conflict arise?

It arises in the application of primary conceptions to particular facts; when for instance one says, 'He has done well: he is brave,' and another, 'Nay, he is out of his mind.' Hence arises the conflict of men with one another. Such is the conflict between Jews and Syrians and Egyptians and Romans–not the question whether holiness must be put before all things and must in all circumstances be pursued, but whether it is holy or unholy to eat of swine's flesh. Such you will find is the conflict between Agamemnon and Achilles. Call them to come forward.

What do you say, Agamemnon? Do you say that what is right and noble ought not to be done?

'Of course it ought.'

And what do you say, Achilles? Do you not approve of doing what is noble?

'Nay, I approve of it above all things.'

Now apply these primary notions: and here the conflict begins. One says, 'I ought not to give back Chryseis to her father.' The other says, 'Nay, you ought.' Certainly one or other of them wrongly applies the primary notion of right. Again one says, 'Well, if I must give back Chryseis, I must take the prize from one of you': the other says, 'What, take away my beloved?' 'Yes, yours,' he says. 'Am I alone then to be the loser?' 'But am I alone to have nothing?' So a conflict arises.

In what then does education consist? In learning to apply the natural primary conceptions to particular occasions in accordance with nature, and further to distinguish between things in our power and things not in our power. In our power are will and all operations of the will, and beyond our power are the body, the parts of the body, possessions, parents, brothers, children, country, in a word–those whose society we share. Where then are we to place 'the good'? To what class of things shall we apply it?

'To what is in our power.'

Does it follow then that health and a whole body, and life are not good, nor children, parents, and country? No one will bear with you if you say that. Let us then transfer the name 'good' to this class of things. Is it possible for a man to be happy if he is injured and fails to win good things?

'It is impossible.'

Can he also find the proper way to live with his fellows? Nay, how is it possible? For instance, I incline by nature to my true interest. If it is my interest to have a field, it is also my interest to take it away from my neighbour: if it is my interest to have a robe, it is my interest also to steal it from the bath. This is the source of wars, factions, tyrannies, plots.

Again, how shall I be able to observe what is fitting towards Zeus, for if I am injured or unfortunate, he heeds me not? So one hears, 'What have I to do with him, if he cannot help me?' and again, 'What have I to do with him, if he wills that I should be as I am now?' It follows that I begin to hate him. Why then do we build temples and make images to Zeus as if he were an evil genius, as if he were Fever? How can we give him any more the name Saviour, Rain-giver, and Fruit-giver? Surely if we place the true nature of the good in outward things, all these consequences follow.

What are we to do then? This is the search to be made by the true student of philosophy, who is in travail with truth. These are his thoughts: 'I do not see what is good and what evil. Am I not mad? I am.' But if I put 'the good' in the region of things that my will controls, every one will laugh at me. Some grey-haired old man will arrive, with many gold rings on his fingers: then he will shake his head and say, 'Listen to me, my child: you must study philosophy, but you must keep a cool head too. All that talk is folly. You learn the syllogism from philosophers, but you know better than the philosophers what you ought to do.'

Fellow, why do you rebuke me then, if I know it? What am I to say to this slave? If I am silent, he bursts with anger. One ought to say, 'Pardon me as you would pardon lovers. I am not my own master. I am mad.'

CHAPTER TWENTY THREE

Against Epicurus

EPICURUS UNDERSTANDS as well as we do that we are by nature social beings, but having once placed our good not in the spirit but in the husk which contains it he cannot say anything different. On the other hand he firmly grasps the principle that one must not admire nor accept anything which is severed from the nature of the good: and he is quite right.

How can we be social beings, if (as you say) we have no natural affection for our offspring? Why do you advise the wise man not to bring up children? Why are you afraid that they may bring him into troubles?

Does the mouse he rears indoors cause him trouble? What does he care then, if a tiny mouse begins crying in his house? But he knows that if once a child is born, it will not be in our power not to love it nor care for it.

Epicurus says that the man who is wise does not enter into politics, for he knows what sort of things the politician has to do. Of course if you are going to live among men as if they were flies, what is to prevent you? But Epicurus, as though he did not know what natural affection is, says 'Let us not bring up children.'

If a sheep does not abandon its offspring, nor a wolf, does a man abandon his? What would you have us do? Would you have us foolish as sheep? Even they do not abandon their young. Would you have us savage as wolves? Even they do not abandon theirs. Nay, who takes your advice when he sees his child fallen on the ground and crying? Why, I think that if your father and mother had foreseen that you were going to talk thus, even then they would not have cast you away from them.

CHAPTER TWENTY FOUR

How One should Contend against Difficulties

DIFFICULTIES ARE WHAT SHOW men's character. Therefore when a difficult crisis meets you, remember that you are as the raw youth with whom God the trainer is wrestling.

'To what end?' the hearer asks.

That you may win at Olympia: and that

cannot be done without sweating for it. To my mind no man's difficulties ever gave him a finer trial than yours, if only you will use them for exercise, as the athlete wrestles with the young man. Even now we are sending you to Rome to spy out the land: and no one sends a coward as a spy, for that means that if he but hears a noise or sees a shadow anywhere, he will come running in confusion and saying that the enemy are close at hand. So now if you come and tell us 'The doings in Rome are fearful, death is terrible, exile is terrible, evil-speaking is terrible, poverty is terrible: fly sirs, the enemy is at hand', we shall say to you, 'Begone, prophesy to yourself, the only mistake we made was in sending a man like you to spy out the land'. Diogenes, who was sent scouting before you, has brought us back a different report: he says, 'Death is not evil, for it is not dishonour'; he says, 'Glory is a vain noise made by madmen'. And what a message this scout brought us about pain and pleasure and poverty! 'To wear no raiment', he says, 'is better than any robe with purple hem'; 'to sleep on the ground without a bed', he says, 'is the softest couch.' Moreover he proves each point by showing his own confidence, his tranquillity of mind, his freedom, and withal his body well knit, and in good condition. 'No enemy is near,' he says, 'all is full of peace.'

What do you mean, Diogenes?

'See,' he says, 'have I suffered shot or wound or rout?'

That is the right kind of scouting: but you come back to us and talk at random. Drop your cowardice and go back again, and take a more accurate observation.

What am I to do then?

What do you do, when you disembark from a ship? Do you take the helm and the oars with you? What do you take then? You take what is yours, oil-flask and wallet. So now if you remember what is yours, you will never claim what is another's.

The emperor says to you, 'Lay aside your purple hem.'

See, I wear the narrow one.

'Lay aside this also.'

See, I wear the toga only.

'Lay aside the toga.'

See, I take that off too.

'Ay, but you still rouse my envy.'

Then take my poor body, every bit of it. The man to whom I can throw away my body has no fears for me.

'But he will not leave me as his heir.'

What? Did I forget that none of these things was mine? In what sense do we call them 'mine'? Only as we call 'mine' the pallet in an inn. If then the inn-keeper dies and leaves you the pallets, well and good; if he leaves them to another, that man will have them, and you will look for another. If you do not find one you will sleep on the ground, only do so with a good cheer, snoring the while, and remembering that it is among rich men and kings and emperors that tragedies find room, and that no poor man fills a part in a tragedy except as one of the chorus. But kings begin with a prelude of good things:

Crown high the halls

[Author unknown]

and then about the third or fourth act comes–

O Cithaeron, why didst thou receive me?

[Sophocles, **Oedipus the King**, 1391]

Poor slave, where are your crowns, where your diadem? Your guards avail you naught. Therefore when you come near to one of those great men remember this, that you are meeting a tragic character, no actor, but Oedipus in person.

'Nay, but such a one is blessed, for he has a great company to walk with him.'

I too join the ranks of the multitude and have a large company to walk with.

To sum up: remember that the door is

open. Do not be a greater coward than the children, but do as they do. Children, when things do not please them, say, ‘I will not play any more’; so, when things seem to you to reach that point, just say, ‘I will not play any more,’ and so depart, instead of staying to make moan.

CHAPTER TWENTY FIVE

On the Same Theme

IF THIS IS TRUE, and if we are not silly and insincere when we say that for men good and evil lies in the region of the will, and that everything else has no concern for us, why are we disturbed or fearful any more? No one has authority over the things in which we are interested: and we pay no regard to the things over which others have authority. What more have we to trouble about?

'Nay, but give me commands' (says the student).

What command should I give you? Has not Zeus laid commands upon you? Has He not given you what is yours, free from hindrance and constraint, and what is not yours subject to hindrance and constraint? What command then have you brought with you into the world, and what manner of ordinance? Guard what is your own by all means, grasp not at the things of others. Your good faith is your own.... Who can take these qualities from you? Who shall hinder you from using them but yourself? And how will you do so? When you take no interest in what is your own, you lose it and it ceases to be yours.

When you have instructions and commands from Zeus such as these, what commands would you have from me? Am I greater or more trustworthy than He? Do you need any other commands if you keep these of His?

Has He not laid these commands upon you? Look at the primary conceptions. Look at the demonstrations of philosophers. Look at the lessons you have often heard, and the words you have spoken yourself–all you have read, all you have studied.

How long, then, is it right to keep these commands and not break up the game?

As long as it is conducted properly.

Here is a king chosen by lot at the Saturnalia: for they decide to play the game of 'Kings'. He gives his orders: '**You** drink, **you** mix the wine, **you** sing, **you** go, **you** come'. I obey, that I may not break up the game.

'Now believe that you are in evil case.'

I do not believe it, and who will compel me to believe it?

Again, we agree to play 'Agamemnon and Achilles'. He who is given the part of Agamemnon says to me, 'Go to Achilles and drag away Briseis'. I go. 'Come.' I come.

In fact we must behave in life as we do with hypothetical arguments. 'Let us assume it is night.'

Granted.

'What follows? Is it day?'

No, for I have already assented to the assumption that it is night.

'Let us assume that you believe that it is night.'

Granted.

'Now believe that it really is night.'

This does not follow from the hypothesis.

So too it is in life. 'Let us assume that you are unfortunate.'

Granted.

'Are you then unfortunate?'

Yes.

'What then, are you in misery?'

Yes.

'Now, believe that you are in evil case.'

This does not follow from the hypothesis: and Another forbids me.

How far, then, must we submit to such commands? So far as is expedient; that is, so far as I am true to what is becoming and consistent. There are, however, some severe and sour-tempered persons who say, 'I cannot dine with this fellow, and put up with his daily narrative of how he fought in Mysia. "I told you, brother, how I mounted the hill: now I begin again at the siege."' Another says, 'I would rather dine and hear him babble on to his heart's content.' It is for you to compare these estimates: only do nothing in the spirit of one burdened and afflicted, who believes himself in evil case: for no one compels you to this. Suppose some one made the room smoke. If the smoke is moderate I will stay: if excessive, I go out: for one must remember and hold fast to this, that the door is open.

The order comes, 'Do not dwell in Nicopolis.'

I will not.

'Nor in Athens.'

I give up Athens.

'Nor in Rome.'

I give up Rome.

'Dwell in Gyara.'

I dwell in Gyara: but this seems to me a very smoky room indeed, and I depart where no one shall hinder me from dwelling: for that dwelling is open to every man. And beyond the last inner tunic, which is this poor body of mine, no one has any authority over me at all. That is why Demetrius said to Nero, 'You threaten me with death, but nature threatens you.' If I pay regard to my poor body, I have given myself over as a slave: and if I value my wretched property I am a slave, for thereby I show at once what power can master me. Just as when the snake draws in its head I say, 'Strike the part of him which he guards,' so you may be sure that your master will trample on that part of you which you wish to guard. When you remember this, whom will you flatter or fear any more?

'Nay, but I want to sit where the senators sit.'

Do you see that you are making a strait

place for yourself and squeezing yourself?

'How else then shall I have a good view in the amphitheatre?'

Man, do not go to the show and you will not be crushed. Why do you trouble yourself? Or wait a little, and when the show is done, sit down in the senators' seats and sun yourself. For remember this (and it is true universally) that it is we who straiten and crush ourselves–that is to say, it is our judgements which straiten and crush us. For instance, what does it mean to be slandered? Stand by a stone and slander it: what effect will you produce? If a man then listens like a stone, what advantage has the slanderer? But if the slanderer has the weakness of him that he slanders to work upon, then he does achieve something.

'Tear his toga off him.'

Why bring **him** in? Take his toga. Tear that.

'I have done you an outrage.'

May it turn out to your good.

These were the principles that. Socrates

practised: that is why his face always wore the same expression. But we are fain to study and practise everything except how to be free men and untrammelled.

'The philosophers talk paradoxes.'

But are there no paradoxes in the other arts? Nay, what is more paradoxical than to lance a man's eye that he may see? If one told this to a person unskilled in the physician's art, would he not laugh at him who said it? Is it surprising then that in philosophy also many truths seem paradoxical to those who are unskilled?

CHAPTER TWENTY SIX

What is the Law of Life

WHEN SOME ONE WAS reciting hypothetical arguments, Epictetus said: This also is a law which governs hypothesis, that we must accept what conforms with the hypothesis. But much more important is the law of living, which is this–to act in conformity with nature. For if we wish in every subject and in all circumstances to observe what is natural, it is plain that in everything we must aim at not letting slip what is in harmony with nature nor accepting what is in conflict with it. First, then, philosophers train us in the region of speculation, which is easier, and only then lead us on to what is harder: for in the sphere of speculation there is no influence which hinders us from following what we are taught, but in life there are many influences which drag us the contrary way. We may laugh, then, at him who says that he wants to try living first; for it is not easy to begin with what is harder.

And this is the defence that we must plead with parents who are angered at their children studying philosophy: 'Suppose I am in error, my father, and ignorant of what is fitting and proper for me. If, then, this cannot be taught or learnt, why do you reproach me? If it can be taught, teach me, and, if you cannot, let me learn from those who say that they know. For what think you? That I fall into evil and fail to do well because I wish to? God forbid. What, then, is the cause of my going wrong? Ignorance. Would you not then have me put away my ignorance? Who was ever taught the art of music or of steering by anger? Do you think, then, that your anger will enable me to learn the art of living?' This argument can only be used by one who has entertained the purpose of right living. But if a man studies logic and goes to the philosophers just because he wants to show at a dinner party that he knows hypothetical arguments, is he not merely trying to win the admiration of some senator who sits next him? For in such society the great forces of the world prevail, and what we call wealth here seems child's-play there.

This is what makes it difficult to get the mastery over one's impressions, where distracting forces are strong. I know a man who clung to the knees of Epaphroditus in tears and said he was in distress, for he had nothing left but a million and a half.

What did Epaphroditus do? Did he laugh at him, as we should? No, he was astonished, and said, 'Unhappy man, how ever did you manage to keep silence and endure it?'

Once when he put to confusion the student who was reading hypothetical arguments, and the master who had set him to read laughed at his pupil, he said, You are laughing at yourself; you did not give the young man any preliminary training, nor discover whether he can follow the arguments, but just treat him as a reader. Why is it, he said, that when a mind is unable to follow and judge a complex argument we trust to it the task of praise and blame and of deciding on good and bad actions? If he speaks ill of any one, does the man attend to him, and is any one elated by a praise which comes from one who cannot find the logical connexion in such small matters?

This, then, is where the philosophic life begins; in the discovery of the true state of one's own mind: for when once you realize that it is in a feeble state, you will not choose to employ it any more for great matters. But, as it is, some men, finding themselves unable to swallow a mouthful, buy themselves a treatise, and set about eating it whole, and, in consequence they vomit or have indigestion. Hence come colics and fluxes and fevers. They ought first to have considered whether they have the faculty.

It is easy enough in speculation to examine and refute the ignorant, but in practical life men do not submit themselves to be tested, and we hate the man who examines and exposes us. Yet Socrates used to say that a life which was not put to the test was not worth living. [Plato, **Apology**, 38a]

CHAPTER TWENTY SEVEN

On the Ways in which Impressions Come to us: And the Aids we must Provide for Ourselves to Deal with them

IMPRESSIONS COME TO US in four ways: either things are and seem so to us; or they are not and seem not to be; or they are and seem not; or they are not and yet seem to be. Now it is the business of the true philosopher to deal rightly with all these; he ought to afford help at whatever point the pressure comes. If it is the fallacies of Pyrrho and of the Academy which crush us, let us render help against them. If it is the plausibilities of circumstances, which make things seem good which are not, let us seek help against this danger: if it is habit which crushes us, we must try to discover help against that.

What, then, can we discover to help us against habit?

Contrary habit.

You hear ignorant folk saying, 'Unhappy man that he was, he died': 'His father perished, and his mother': 'He was cut off, yes, and untimely and in a foreign land.' Now listen to the arguments on the other side; draw yourself away from these voices, set against habit the opposite habit. Set against fallacious arguments the processes of reason, training yourself to be familiar with these processes: against the plausibilities of things we must have our primary conceptions clear, like weapons bright and ready for use.

When death appears an evil we must have ready to hand the argument that it is fitting to avoid evils, and death is a necessary thing. What am I to do? Where am I to escape it? Grant that I am not Sarpedon son of Zeus, to utter those noble words, 'I would fain go and achieve glory or afford another the occasion to achieve it: if I cannot win success myself, I will not grudge another the chance of doing a noble deed'. Grant that this is beyond us, can we not compass the other?

I ask you, Where am I to escape death? Point me to the place, point me to the people, among whom I am to go, on whom it does not light, point me to a charm against it. If I have none, what would you have me do? I cannot escape death: am I not to escape the fear of it? Am I to die in tears and trembling? For trouble of mind springs from this, from wishing for a thing which does not come to pass. Wheresoever I can alter external things to suit my own will, I alter them: where I cannot, I am fain to tear any man's eyes out who stands in my way. For man's nature is such that he cannot bear to be deprived of what is good, nor can he bear to be involved in evil. And so the end of the matter is that when I cannot alter things, nor blind him that hinders me, I sit still and moan and revile whom I can–Zeus and the other gods; for if they heed me not, what have I to do with them?

'Yes, but that will be impious of you.'

Well, how shall I be worse off than I am now? In a word, we must remember this, that unless piety and true interest coincide, piety cannot be preserved in a man. Do not these principles seem to you to be urgent?

Let the Pyrrhonist and the disciple of the Academy come and maintain the contrary! For my part I have no leisure for these discussions, nor can I act as advocate to the common-sense view.

If I had some petty action concerned with a plot of land, I should have called in another to be my advocate, how much more in a matter of this concern.

With what argument, then, am I content? With what is appropriate to the subject in hand. How sensation takes place, whether through the whole body or through particular parts, I cannot render a reasoned account, though I find difficulty in both views. But that you and I are not the same persons, I know absolutely and for certain. How is that? When I want to swallow a morsel I never lift it to your mouth, but to mine. When I want to take a piece of bread, I never take rubbish instead, but go to the bread as to a mark. And even you who make nothing of the senses, act just as I do. Which of you when he wants to go to the bath goes to the mill instead?

What follows? Must we not to the best of our power hold fast to this –that is, maintain the view of common sense, and guard ourselves against all that upsets it? Yes, who disputes that? But these are matters for one who has the power and the leisure: the man who trembles, and is disturbed, and whose heart is shaken within him, ought to devote his time to something else.

CHAPTER TWENTY EIGHT

That we must not be Angry with Men: And Concerning what Things are Small and What are Great among Men

WHAT IS THE REASON that we assent to a thing? Because it seems to us that it is so. It is impossible that we shall assent to that which seems not to be. Why? Because this is the nature of the mind–to agree to what is true, and disagree with what is false, and withhold judgement on what is doubtful.

What is the proof of this?

'Feel now, if you can, that it is night.'

It is impossible.

Put away the feeling that it is day.'

It is impossible.

'Assume or put away the feeling that the stars are even in number.' It is not possible.

When a man assents, then, to what is false, know that he had no wish to assent to the false: 'for no soul is robbed of the truth with its own consent,' as Plato says, but the false seemed to him true.

Now, in the sphere of action what have we to correspond to true and false in the sphere of perception? What is fitting and unfitting, profitable and unprofitable, appropriate and inappropriate, and the like.

Cannot a man, then, think a thing is to his profit, and not choose it?

He cannot.

What of her who says

I know full well what ills I mean to do
But passion overpowers what counsel bids me.

[Euripides, **Medea**, 1078]

Here the very gratification of passion and the vengeance she takes on her husband she believes to be more to her profit than saving her children.

'Yes, but she is deceived.'

Prove to her plainly that she is deceived and she will not do it, but as long as you do not show her, what else can she follow but that which appears to her? Nothing. Why then are you indignant with her, because, unhappy woman, she is deluded on the greatest matters and is transformed from a human being into a serpent? Why do you not rather pity her–if so it may be? As we pity the blind and the lame, so should we pity those who are blinded and lamed in their most sovereign faculties.

We must remember this clearly, that man measures his every action by his impressions; of course they may be good or bad: if good, he is free from reproach; if bad, he pays the penalty in his own person, for it is impossible for one to be deluded and another to suffer for it. The man who remembers this, I say, will be angry with no one, indignant with no one, revile none, blame none, hate none, offend none.

'So you say that deeds so great and awful take their origin from this, the impressions of the mind?'

From this and nothing else. The Iliad is nothing but men's impressions and how they dealt with them. It was impressions that made Paris take away the wife of Menelaus, impressions that drew Helen to follow him. If, then, his impressions had led Menelaus to feel that it was a gain to be robbed of such a wife, what would have happened? We should have lost the Iliad, and not only that but the Odyssey too.

'What? Do these great matters depend on one that is so small?'

What are these you call 'such great matters'? Wars and factions, deaths of many men and destructions of cities. What is there great in this, pray?

'Is there nothing great?'

Why, what is there great in the death of many oxen and many sheep, and the burning and destruction of many nests of swallows and storks? 'Are these like those other horrors?'

Most like: bodies of men perished, so did bodies of oxen and sheep. Huts of men were burnt: so were storks' nests. What is great or awful here? Or if it be so, show me how a man's home differs from a stork's nest, as a dwelling.

'Is a stork, then, like a man?'

What do you say? In respect of his body, very like; save only that men's homes are built of beams and rafters and bricks, and storks' nests of sticks and clay.

'Does a man then differ in nothing from a stork?'

God forbid: but he does not differ in these matters.

'In what then does he differ?'

Search and you will find that he differs in something else. Look whether it be not that he differs in understanding what he does, in his faculty for society, in his good faith, his self-respect, his security of aim, his prudence.

Where then is man's good and man's evil, in the true sense, to be found?

In that faculty which makes men different from all else. If a man preserves this and keeps it safely fortified; if his sense of honour, his good faith, and his prudence are not destroyed, then he too is preserved; but if any of these perish or be taken by storm, then he too perishes with them. And it is on this that great events depend. Was Alexander's great failure when the Hellenes came against the Trojans and sacked Troy and when his brothers perished? By no means: for no one fails by the act of another; yet then there was destruction of storks' nests. Nay, his failure was when he lost the man of honour, the man of good faith, the man who respected manners and the laws of hospitality. When did Achilles fail? Was it when Patroclus died? God forbid: it was when he was angry, when he cried for a trumpery maiden, when he forgot that he was there not to win lady-loves, but to make war. These are man's failures–this is his siege, this is his razed city, when his right judgements are broken to the ground, and when they are destroyed.

'But when women are carried off, and children are made captive, and men themselves are slaughtered–are not these things evil?'

Where do you get this idea from? If it is true, teach it me too.

'No, I cannot: but how can you say that they are not evil?'

Let us turn to our standards, let us look to our primary notions. For I cannot be sufficiently astonished at what men do. When we want to judge weights, we do not judge at random: when we judge things straight and crooked, it is not at random: in a word, when it is important to us to know the truth on any subject, no one of us will ever do anything at random. Yet when we are dealing with the primary and sole cause of right or wrong action, of prosperity or adversity, of good or bad fortune, there alone we are random and headlong: we nowhere have anything like a scale, nowhere anything like a standard: some impression strikes me, and straightway I act on it.

Am I any better than Agamemnon or Achilles, that they should do and suffer such evils because they follow their impressions, and I should be content with mine?

Surely tragedy has no other source but this. What is the 'Atreus' of Euripides? Impressions. What is the 'Oedipus' of

Sophocles? Impressions. 'Phoenix'? Impressions. 'Hippolytus'? Impressions. How do you think then we should describe the man who takes no pains to discipline his impressions? What name do we give to those who follow everything that comes into their mind?

'Madmen.'

Well, is not this exactly what we do?

CHAPTER TWENTY NINE

On Constancy

THE ESSENCE OF GOOD and of evil lies in an attitude of the will. What are external things then?

They are materials for the will, in dealing with which it will find its own good or evil.

How will it find its good?

If it does not value over much the things that it deals with. For its judgements on matters presented to it, if they be right, make the will good, and if crooked and perverse make it bad. This law God has ordained and says, 'If you want anything good, get it from yourself.'

You say, 'Not so, but from another.'

I say, No, from yourself. So when the tyrant threatens and does not invite me, I say, 'What does he threaten?' If he says, 'I will bind you', I say, 'He threatens my hands and my feet.' If he says, 'I will behead you', I say, 'He threatens my neck'. If he says, 'I will put you in prison', I say, 'He threatens all my poor flesh', and if he threatens banishment, the same.

'Does he then not threaten you at all?'

Not at all, if I feel that these things are nothing to me: but if I fear any of them, he does threaten me. Who is there left for me to fear, and over what has he control? Over what is in my power? No one controls that. Over what is not in my power? I have no concern in that.

'Do you philosophers then teach us to despise kings?'

Heaven forbid! Which of us teaches men to resist them in the matters over which they have authority? Take my bit of a body, take my property, take my good name, take my companions. If I try to persuade any of them to resist, I give him leave to accuse me indeed.

'Yes, but I want to command your judgements.'

Who has given you this authority? How can you conquer another's judgement?

'I will conquer him', he says, 'by bringing fear to bear on him.'

You are not aware that it was the judgement that conquered itself, it was not conquered by another. The will may conquer itself, but nothing else can conquer it. That is the reason too why the noblest and most just law of God is this: 'Let the better always be victorious over the worse.'

'Ten', you say, 'are better than one.'

Better for what? To bind, to slay, to carry off where they will, to take away property.

Ten conquer one therefore only in so far as they are better.

'In what then are they worse?'

They are worse if the one has right judgements, and the ten have not. I ask you, can they conquer him in this? How can they? If we weigh them in the balance, must not the heavier pull down the scale?

'This is your outcome then, that Socrates should suffer the fate he did at the hands of the Athenians?'

Slave, why do you say, 'Socrates'? State the fact as it really is, That Socrates' vile body should be arrested and haled to prison by those who are stronger, and that some one should give hemlock to Socrates' vile body and it should die of chill–does this seem to you marvellous, does this seem unjust, is it for this you accuse God? Did Socrates then get nothing in exchange? In what did his true good consist? Which are we to attend to? To you or to him? Nay, what does Socrates say? 'Anytus or Meletus can slay me, but they cannot harm me' [Plato, **Apology**, 30c]: and again, 'If God so will, so be it.' [Plato, **Crito**, 43d] Prove, I say, that one who has worse judgements gains the mastery over him who is his superior in judgements. You will not prove it: far from it. For the law of nature and of God is this, 'Let the better always come out victor over the worse.' Victorious in what? In that wherein it is better. One body is stronger than another, the majority are stronger than one, the thief stronger than he who is not a thief. That is why I too lost my lamp, because in the matter of vigilance the thief was a stronger man than I. But he bought his lamp for this price: for a lamp he became a thief, for a lamp he broke his faith, for a lamp he became a brute. This seemed to his judgement to be profitable.

Very well: but now some one has laid hold on my cloak, and drags me into the market, then others raise a clamour against me, 'Philosopher, what good have your judgements done you? for, see, you are haled to prison, see, you are about to be beheaded.'

And what sort of Introduction to philosophy could I have studied, that would save me from being haled off, if a stronger man seizes my cloak, or, if ten men drag me about and cast me into prison, will save me from being cast there? Have I then learnt nothing else? I have learnt to see that everything that happens, if it is beyond the control of my will, is nothing to me. Have you not gained benefit then in this respect? Why do you seek benefit elsewhere than where you learnt that it is to be found?

I sit on then in prison and say, 'This person who clamours at me has no ear for the true meaning of things, he does not understand what is said, in a word he has taken no pains to know what philosophers do or say. Let him be.'

But the answer comes, 'Come out of your prison.'

If you have no more need of me in prison, I

come out: if you need me again, I will come in. For how long? For as long as reason requires that I should abide by my vile body; but when reason demands it no longer, take it from me and good health to you! Only let me not cast it off without reason or from a faint heart, or for a casual pretext. For again God wills it not: for He has need of a world like this, and of such creatures as ourselves to move upon the earth. But if He give the signal of retreat, as He gave it to Socrates, one must obey His signal as that of the general in command.

'What then? must I say these things to the multitude?'

Why should you? Is it not sufficient to believe them yourself? For when children come up to us and clap their hands and say, 'A good Saturnalia to you to-day!' do we say 'These things are not good'? Not at all, we clap with them ourselves. So, when you cannot change a man's opinion, recognize that he is a child, clap with him, and if you do not wish to do this, you have only to hold your peace.

These things we must remember, and when called to face a crisis that is to test us we must realize that the moment is come to show whether we have learnt our lesson. For a young man going straight from his studies to face a crisis may be compared to one who has practised the analysis of syllogisms. If some one offers him one that is easy to analyse, he says, 'Nay, propound me one which is cunningly involved, that I may get proper exercise.' And so wrestlers are discontented if put to wrestle with young men of light weight: 'He cannot lift me', one says. Here is a young man of parts, yet when the crisis calls he must needs weep and say, 'I would fain go on learning.'

Learning what? If you did not learn your lesson to display it in action, what did you learn it for?

I imagine one of those who are sitting here crying out in the travail of his heart, 'Why does not a crisis come to me such as has come to him? Am I to wear my life out idly in a corner, when I might win a crown at Olympia? When will some one bring me news of a contest like that?' Such ought to be the attitude of you all. Why, among Caesar's gladiators there are some who are vexed that no one brings them out or matches them in fight, and they pray to God and go to the managers and implore them to let them fight; and shall no one of you display a like spirit? That is exactly why I should like to take ship for Rome to see how my wrestler puts his lesson into practice.

'I do not want', says he, 'an exercise of this sort.'

What? is it in your power to take the task you choose? No, a body is given you of such a kind, parents of such a kind, brothers of such a kind, a country of such a kind, a position in it of such a kind: and yet you come to me and say, 'Change the task set me.' What! have you not resources, to deal with what is given you? Instead of saying, 'It is yours to set the task, and mine to study it well', you say, 'Do not put before me such a syllogism, but such an one: do not impose on me such a conclusion, but such an one.' A time will soon come when tragic actors will imagine that they are merely mask and shoes and robe, and nothing else. Man, you have these things given you as your subject and task. Speak your pan, that we may know whether you are a tragic actor or a buffoon: for except their speech they have all else in common. Does the tragic actor disappear, if you take away his shoes and mask and bring him on the stage in the bare guise of a ghost, or is he there still? If he has a voice he is there still.

So it is in life: 'Take a post of command'; I take it, and taking it show how a philosopher behaves.

'Lay aside the senator's dress, and put on rags and appear in that character.' Very well: is it not given me still to display a noble voice? In what part then do you appear now?

As a witness called by God: 'Come and bear witness for me, for I count you worthy to come forward as my witness. Is anything good or evil which lies outside the range of the will? Do I harm any one? Do I put each man's advantage elsewhere than in himself?'

What is the witness you now bear to God?

'I am in danger, O Lord, and in misfortune; no man heeds me, no man gives me anything, all blame me and speak evil of me.'

Is this the witness you are going to bear, and so dishonour the calling that he has given you, in that he honoured you thus and counted you worthy to be brought forward to bear such weighty witness?

But suppose that he who has authority pronounces, 'I judge you to be godless and unholy', how does this affect you?

'I am judged to be godless and unholy.'

Nothing more?

'Nothing.'

If he had been giving judgement on a hypothetical proposition and had declared, 'I judge the proposition "if it be day, there is light" to be false', how would it have affected the proposition? Who is judged here? Who is condemned? The proposition or the man who is deluded about it? Who in the world then is this who has authority to pronounce upon you? Does he know what godliness or ungodliness is? Has he made a study of it? Has he learnt it? Where and with what master? If a musician pays no heed to him when he pronounces that the lowest note is the highest, nor a geometrician when he decides that the lines from the centre of a circle to the circumference are not equal, shall he who is educated in true philosophy pay any heed to an uneducated man when he gives judgement on what is holy and unholy, just and unjust? What a great wrong for philosophers to be guilty of! Is this what you have learnt by coming to school?

Leave other people, persons of no endurance, to argue on these matters to little purpose. Let them sit in a corner and take their paltry fees, or murmur that no one offers them anything, and come forward yourself and practise what you have learnt. For it is not arguments that are wanting nowadays: no, the books of the Stoics are full of them. What then is the one thing wanting? We want the man who will apply his arguments, and bear witness to them by action. This is the character I would have you take up, that we may no longer make use of old examples in the school, but may be able to show an example from our own day.

Whose business then is it to take cognizance of these questions? It is for him that has studied at school; for man is a creature with a faculty of taking cognizance, but it is shameful for him to exercise it in the spirit of runaway slaves. No: one must sit undistracted and listen in turn to tragic actor or harp-player, and not do as the runaways do. At the very moment one of them is attending and praising the actor, he gives a glance all round, and then if some one utters the word 'master' he is fluttered and confounded in a moment. It is shameful that philosophers should take cognizance of the works of nature in this spirit. For what does 'master' mean? No man is master of another man; his masters are only death and life, pleasure and pain. For, apart from them, you may bring me face to face with Caesar and you shall see what constancy I show. But when he comes in thunder and lightning with these in his train, and I show fear of them, I am only recognizing my master as the runaway does. But so long as I have respite from them I am just like the runaway watching in the theatre; I wash, drink, sing, but do everything in fear and misery. But if I once free myself from my masters, that is from those feelings which make masters formidable, my trouble is past, and I have a master no more.

'Should I then proclaim this to all men?'

No! One should study the weakness of the uninstructed and say to them, 'This man advises me what he thinks good for himself, and I excuse him.' For Socrates too excused the gaoler who wept when he was going to drink the poison, and said, 'How nobly he has wept for us!' Does he say to the gaoler, 'That is why we dismissed the women'? No, he says that to his intimate friends, who were fit to hear it, but the gaoler he treats considerately like a child. [Plato, **Phaedo**, 116d]

CHAPTER THIRTY

What a Man should have Ready to Hand in the Crises of Life

WHEN YOU APPEAR BEFORE one of the mighty of the earth, remember that Another looks from above on what is happening and that you must please Him rather than this man. He that is above inquires of you: 'What did you say in the school about exile and prison and bonds and death and dishonour?'

I said they were ‘indifferent’.

‘What do you call them now, then? Have they changed?’

No.

‘Have you changed then?’

No.

‘Tell me then what things are indifferent.’

Things which lie outside the will’s control.

‘Tell me what follows.’

Things indifferent concern me not at all.

‘Tell me also what you thought were “good things”.’

A right will and a faculty of dealing rightly with impressions. ‘And what did you think was the end?’

To follow Thee.

‘Do you still say that?’

Yes. I say the same now as before.

Go on then into the palace in confidence and remember these things, and you shall see how a young man who has studied what he ought compares with men who have had no study. By the gods I imagine that you will feel thus: 'Why do we make these many and great preparations for nothing? Is this what authority meant? Are the vestibule, the chamberlains, the guards no more than this? Was it for this that I listened to those long discourses? These terrors were naught, and I made ready for them all the time as though they were great matters.'

BOOK TWO

CHAPTER ONE

On Things in our Power and Things not in our Power

PERHAPS THE CONTENTION OF philosophers that it is possible in everything we do to combine confidence with caution may appear a paradox, but nevertheless we must do our best to consider whether it is true. In a sense, no doubt, caution seems to be contrary to confidence, and contraries are by no means compatible. But I think that what seems to many a paradox in this subject depends on a confusion, and it is this. If we really called upon a man to use caution and confidence in regard to the same things, they might fairly find fault with us as uniting qualities which cannot be united. But as a matter of fact there is nothing strange in the statement: for if it is true, as has often been said and often proved, that the true nature of good and also of evil depends on how we deal with impressions, and if things outside the will's control cannot be described as good or bad, we cannot surely call it a paradoxical demand of the philosophers if they say, 'Be confident in all that lies beyond the will's control, be cautious in all that is dependent on the will.' For if evil depends on evil choice, it is only in regard to matters of will that it is right to use caution; and if things outside the will's control, which do not depend on us, concern us in no way, we should use confidence in regard to these. And in that way we shall be at once cautious and confident and indeed confident because of our caution. For because we are cautious as to things which are really evil we shall get confidence to face things which are not so.

However, we behave like deer: when hinds fear the feathers and fly from them, where do they turn, and in what do they take refuge as a safe retreat? They turn to the nets, and so they perish because they confuse objects of fear with objects of confidence.

So it is with us. Where do we show fear? In regard to things outside our will's control. Again, when do we behave with confidence as though there were nothing to fear? In matters within the will's control. So if only we are successful in things beyond our will's control we think it is of no consequence to us to be deceived or to act rashly, or to do a shameless deed, or to conceive a shameful desire. But where death or exile or pain or infamy confronts us, there we show the spirit of retreat and of wild alarm. Wherefore, as is likely with men who are mistaken in the greatest matters, we convert our natural confidence into something bold, desperate, reckless, shameless, whereas we change our natural caution and modesty into a cowardly and abject quality, full of fears and perturbations. For if a man transfers his caution to the region of the will and the operations of the will, with the will to be cautious he will find that the will to avoid lies in his control: while if he turns his caution to what is beyond the control of our will, inasmuch as his will to avoid will be directed to what depends upon others he will of necessity be subject to fear, inconstancy, and perturbation. For it is not death or pain which is a fearful thing, but the fear of pain or death. Therefore men praise him who said

Not death, but shameful death, is to be feared.

[Author unknown]

We ought then to turn our confidence towards death, and our caution towards the fear of death: what we really do is just the contrary; we fly from death, yet we pay no heed to forming judgements about death, but are reckless and indifferent. Socrates called such fears 'bogies', and rightly too. [Plato, **Phaedo**, 77e] For just as masks seem fearful and terrible to children from want of experience, so we are affected by events for much the same reason as children are affected by 'bogies'. For what makes a child? Want of knowledge. What makes a child? Want of instruction. For so far as a child knows those things he is no worse off than we are. What is death? A bogy. Turn it round and see what it is: you see it does not bite. The stuff of the body was bound to be parted from the airy element, either now or hereafter, as it existed apart from it before. Why then are you vexed if they are parted now? For if not parted now, they will be hereafter. Why so? That the revolution of the universe may be accomplished, for it has need of things present, things future, and things past and done with. What is pain? A bogy. Turn it round and see what it is. The poor flesh is subject to rough movement, then again to smooth. If it is not to your profit, the door stands open: if it is to your profit, bear it. For in every event the door must stand open and then we have no trouble.

What then is the fruit of these judgements? A fruit which must needs be most noble and most becoming to those who are truly being educated –a mind tranquil and fearless and free. For on these matters you must not trust the multitude, who say, 'Only the free may be educated', but rather the philosophers who say, 'Only the educated are free.'

'What do you mean by that?'

I mean this. What else is freedom but power to pass our life as we will?

'True.'

Tell me, fellow men, do you wish to live doing wrong?

'We do not.'

Is no one free who does wrong?

'No one.'

Do you wish to live in fear, in pain, in distress of mind?

'By no means.'

Well, no man who suffers fear or pain or distress of mind is free, but whoever is quit of fears and pains and distresses is by the self-same road quit of slavery. How then shall we go on believing you, dearest lawgivers?

Do we allow none but the free to get education?

Nay! philosophers say that we do not allow any to be free except those whose education is complete: that is, God does not allow it.

'Well then, when a man turns his slave round before the praetor, does he do nothing?'

He does something.

'What?'

He turns his slave round before the praetor.

'Nothing else?'

Yes, he is bound to pay the twentieth for him.

'What follows? Has not the man to whom this is done gained freedom?'

No more than he has gained peace of mind. For do you who can confer this freedom own no master? Have you not a master in money, a girl lover or a boy lover, the tyrant, or a friend of the tyrant? If not, why do you tremble when you go away to face a crisis of this sort? Therefore I say many times over: What you must practise and have at command is to know what you ought to approach with confidence, and what with caution; all that is beyond the control of the will with confidence, and what is dependent on the will with caution.

'But' (says my pupil), 'have I not recited to you? Do you not know what I am doing?'

What are you engaged on? Paltry phrases.

Away with your paltry phrases: show me how you stand in regard to the will to get and the will to avoid: if you do not fail to get what you will, or fall into what you will to avoid. As for those paltry periods, if you have sense you will take them away somewhere or other and make away with them.

'What do you mean? Did not Socrates write?'

Yes, who wrote so much as he? But under what conditions? He could not always have some one at hand examining his judgements or to be examined by him in turn, and therefore be examined and questioned himself and was always putting to trial some primary conception or other in a practical way. This is what a philosopher writes: but paltry phrases and periods he leaves to others, to the stupid or the blessed, those whose peace of mind gives them leisure for study or those who can draw no logical conclusions because of their folly.

To-day, when the crisis calls you, will you go

off and display your recitation and harp on, 'How cleverly I compose dialogues'? Nay, fellow man, make this your object, 'Look how I fail not to get what I will. Look how I escape what I will to avoid. Let death come and you shall know; bring me pains, prison, dishonour, condemnation.' This is the true field of display for a young man come from school. Leave those other trifles to other men; let no one ever hear you say a word on them, do not tolerate any compliments upon them; assume the air of being no one and of knowing nothing. Show that you know this only, how not to fail and how not to fall. Let others practise law-suits, logical puzzles and syllogisms: let your study be how to suffer death, bondage, the rack, exile: let all this be done with confidence and trust in Him who has called you to face them, and judged you worthy of this place you hold, wherein at your appointed post you shall show what is the power of reason, the Governing Principle, when arrayed against forces which are outside the will. And, if you do this, that paradox will no longer seem impossible or paradoxical–that we must show caution and confidence at the same time, confidence in regard to things beyond the will, caution in things which depend on the will.

CHAPTER TWO

On Peace of Mind

CONSIDER, YOU WHO ARE going into court, what you want to maintain and where you want to end: for if you want to maintain your freedom of will in its natural condition, you have all security and facility to do so, and your trouble is over. If you wish to maintain authority over what is in your power and to keep it naturally free, and if you are content with this, what more need you attend to? For who is master of this, who can take it away from you? If you wish to be a man of honour and trust, who will forbid you? If you wish not to be hindered or compelled, what man will compel you to will to get what is against your judgement, and to will to avoid things that you do not think proper to avoid?

What can he do then? He will cause you troubles which seem to you formidable: but how can he make you will to avoid what is done to you? As long then as you retain in your control the will to get and the will to avoid, you need attend to nothing else. This is your introduction, this your narrative, this your proof, this your victory, this your peroration, this your ground of boasting.

That is why Socrates, in reply to one who reminded him to make ready for the court, said: 'Do you not think my whole life is a preparation for this?'

What kind of preparation?

'I have maintained', said he, 'what is my

own.'

What do you mean?

'I never did an unjust act in my private or in my public life.' [Xenophon, **Apologia Socratis**, 2, 3]

But if you wish to keep what is outside you as well–your paltry body, and goods, and reputation–I advise you to begin this moment to make all possible preparation, and further to study the character of your judge and your opponent. If you must clasp his knees, clasp them; if you must weep, then weep; if you must lament, then lament. For when once you allow outward things to dominate what is your own, you had better become a slave and have done with it. Don't be drawn this way and that, wishing to be a slave one moment and free another, but be this or that simply and with all your mind, free or slave, philosopher or unenlightened, a fighting cock of spirit, or one of no spirit; either bear stroke after stroke patiently till you die, or give way at once. Let it not be your lot to suffer many blows and then give way in the end. If such conduct is shameful, get your own mind clear at once: 'Where is the nature of good and evil to be found? Where truth is. Where truth and nature are, there is caution; where truth and nature are, there is confidence.'

For what think you? If Socrates had wished to keep his outward possessions, would he have come forward and said, 'Anytus and Meletus have power to kill me, but not to harm me'? Was he so foolish as not to see that this road leads not to that end, but elsewhere? Why is it then, that he renders no account to his judges, and adds a word of provocation? Just as my friend Heraclitus, when he had an action in Rhodes concerning a plot of land and had pointed out to the judges that his arguments were just, when he came to his peroration said, 'I will not supplicate you, nor do I regard the judgement you will give; it is you who are on your trial rather than I', and so he made an end of the business. You need not speak like that, only do not supplicate. Do not add the words, 'I do not supplicate', unless, as happened to Socrates, the right time has come deliberately to provoke your judges. If, indeed, you are preparing a peroration of this sort, why do you appear in court? Why do you answer the summons? If you wish to be crucified, wait and the cross will come: but if reason requires that you should answer the summons and do your best to persuade the judge, you must act in accordance with this, but always keeping true to yourself.

On this principle it is ridiculous to say, 'Give me advice.' What advice am I to give you? Say rather, 'Enable my mind to adapt itself to the issue, whatever it may be', for the other phrase is as though a man unskilled in writing should say, 'Tell me what to write, when a name is set me to write.' For if I say 'Dion', and then yonder fellow comes forward and sets him the name not of Dion but of Theon, what is to happen? What is he to write? If you have practised writing, you can prepare yourself for anything that is dictated to you. But if you have not practised, what is the good of my making a suggestion? For if circumstances suggest something different, what will you say or what will you do? Remember then this general principle, and you will need no special suggestion. But if you fix your gaze on outward things, you must needs be tossed up and down, at the will of your master. And who is your master? He who has authority over any of those things on which you set your heart or which you will to avoid.

CHAPTER THREE

To those who Commend Persons to Philosophers

THAT IS A GOOD answer of Diogenes to one who asked him for letters of introduction: 'You are a man, and that his eyes will tell him; but whether you are good or bad he will discover, if he has skill to distinguish the good from the bad; and if he has not that skill, he will never discover it, though I should write him ten thousand letters.' A drachma might just as well ask to be introduced to some one in order to be tested. If the man is a judge of silver, you will introduce yourself. We ought, therefore, to have some faculty to guide us in life, as the assayer has in dealing with silver, that I may be able to say as he does, 'Give me any drachma you please, and I will distinguish.' Now I can deal with a syllogism and say, 'Bring any one you like, and I will distinguish between him who can analyse syllogisms and him who cannot.' Why? Because I know how to analyse them: I have the faculty a man must have who is to recognize those who can handle syllogisms aright. But when I have to deal with life, how do I behave? Sometimes I call a thing good, sometimes evil. And the reason is just this, that whereas I have knowledge of syllogisms, I have no knowledge or experience of life.

CHAPTER FOUR

To the Man Caught in Adultery

WHEN EPICTETUS WAS SAYING that man is born for mutual trust, and he who overthrows this overthrows the quality peculiar to man, there came in one of those who are reputed scholars, a man who had once been caught committing adultery in the city. If, said Epictetus, we put away this trust, for which we are born, and plot against our neighbour's wife, what are we doing?

Are we not pulling down and destroying? Whom? The man of trust, of honour, of piety. Is this all? Are we not overthrowing neighbourly feeling, friendship, the city itself? What position are we taking up?

How am I to treat you, my fellow man? As a neighbour? As a friend? Of what kind? As a citizen? What trust am I to put in you? No doubt, if you were a piece of pottery, so cracked that you could not be used for anything, you would be cast out on the dunghill, and no one would stoop to take you thence: what shall we do with you then, if being a man you can fill no place becoming to a man? Granted that you cannot hold the position of a friend, can you hold that of a slave? And who will trust you? Will you not then consent to be cast upon a dunghill yourself as a useless vessel, as a thing for the dunghill?

Will you complain, 'No man pays any attention to me, a man and a scholar'?

Of course, for you are bad and useless.

Wasps might as well be indignant because no one heeds them, but all avoid them and any one who can strikes and crushes them. Your sting is such that you cause pain and trouble to any one you strike with it. What would you have us do to you? There is no place to put you.

What then? Is it not true that 'women are common property by nature'? I agree, for the sucking-pig is the common property of those who are bidden to the feast. Very well, when it has been cut into portions, come, if you see fit, and snatch the portion of the guest who sits next you, steal it secretly or slip your hand over it and taste it, or if you cannot snatch any of the flesh rub your fingers on the fat and lick them. A fine companion you are for a feast or a dinner, worthy of Socrates indeed!

Again, is not the theatre common to all citizens? When they are seated there, come, if you see fit, and turn one of them out. In the same way you may say that women are common property by nature. But when the law-giver, like the giver of the feast, has apportioned them, will you not look for your own portion instead of stealing what is another's and guzzling that?

'Yes, but I am a scholar and understand Archedemus.'

Well then, understand Archedemus, be an adulterer and a man of broken trust, a wolf or an ape instead of a man; for what is there to hinder you?

CHAPTER FIVE

How a Careful Life is Compatible with a Noble Spirit

MATERIAL THINGS ARE INDIFFERENT, but how we handle them is not indifferent.

How then is one to maintain the constant and tranquil mind, and. therewith the careful spirit which is not random or hasty?

You can do it if you imitate those who play dice. Counters and dice are indifferent:

how do I know what is going to turn up? My business is to use what does turn up with diligence and skill. In like manner this is the principal business of life: distinguish between things, weigh them one against the other, and say, 'External things are not in my power, my will is my own. Where am I to seek what is good and what is evil? Within me, among my own possessions.' You must never use the word good or evil or benefit or injury or any such word, in connexion with other men's possessions.

'Do you mean then that outward things are to be used without care?'

By no means. For this again is evil for the will and unnatural to it. They must be used with care, for their use is not a matter of indifference, but at the same time with constancy and tranquillity, for in themselves they are indifferent. For where the true value of things is concerned, no one can hinder or compel me. I am subject to hindrance and compulsion only in matters which lie out of my power to win, which are neither good nor evil, but they may be dealt with well or ill, and this rests with me.

It is difficult to unite and combine these qualities–the diligence of a man who devotes himself to material things, and the constancy of one who disregards them–yet not impossible. Otherwise it would be impossible to be happy. We act very much as if we were on a voyage. What can I do? I can choose out the helmsman, the sailors, the day, the moment. Then a storm arises. What do I care? I have fulfilled my task: another has now to act, the helmsman. Suppose even the ship goes down. What have I to do then? I do only what lies in my power, drowning, if drown I must, without fear, not crying out or accusing heaven, for I know that what is born must needs also perish. For I am not immortal, but a man, a part of the universe as an hour is part of the day. Like the hour I must be here and like an hour pass away. What matters it then to me how I pass, by drowning or by fever, for by some such means I must needs pass away?

You will see that those who play ball with skill behave so. No one of them discusses whether the ball is good or bad, but only how to strike it and how to receive it. Therefore balanced play consists in this–skill, speed, good judgement consist in this–that while I cannot catch the ball, even if I spread my gown for it, the expert catches it if I throw it. But if we catch or strike the ball with flurry or fear, what is the good of the game? How will any one stick to the game and see how it works out? One will say, 'Strike', and another, 'Do not strike', and another, 'You have had one stroke.' This surely is fighting instead of playing.

In that sense Socrates knew how to play the game.

'What do you mean?'

He knew how to play in the court. 'Tell me, Anytus,' said he, 'in what way you say that

I disbelieve in God. What do you think that divinities are? Are they not either children of the gods, or the mixed offspring of men and gods?' And when Anytus agreed, he said, 'Who then do you think can believe in the existence of mules and not in asses?' [Plato, **Apology**, 27c] He was like one playing at ball. What then was the ball that he played with? Life, imprisonment, exile, taking poison, being deprived of his wife, leaving his children orphans. These were the things he played with, but none the less he played and tossed the ball with balance. So we ought to play the game, so to speak, with all possible care and skill, but treat the ball itself as indifferent. A man must certainly cultivate skill in regard to some outward things: he need not accept a thing for its own sake, but he should show his skill in regard to it, whatever it be. In the same way the weaver does not make fleeces, but devotes himself to dealing with them in whatever form he receives them. Sustenance and property are given you by Another, who can take them away from you too, yes and your bit of a body as well.

It is for you, then, to take what is given you and make the most of it. Then if you come off without harm, others who meet you will rejoice with you in your safety, but the man who has a good eye for conduct, if he sees that you behaved here with honour, will praise you and rejoice with you: but if he sees a man has saved his life by acting dishonourably, he will do the opposite. For where a man can rejoice with reason, his neighbour can rejoice with him also.

How is it then that some external things are described as natural and some as unnatural? It is because we regard ourselves as detached from the rest of the universe. For the foot (for instance), I shall say it is natural to be clean, but if you take it as a foot and not as a detached thing, it will be fitting for it to walk in the mud and tread upon thorns and sometimes to be cut off for the sake of the whole body: or else it will cease to be a foot. We must hold exactly the same sort of view about ourselves.

What are you? A man. If you regard man as a detached being, it is natural for him to live to old age, to be rich, to be healthy. But if you regard him as a man and a part of a larger whole, that whole makes it fitting that at one moment you should fall ill, at another go a voyage and risk your life, and at another be at your wit's end, and, it may be, die before your time. Why then are you indignant? Do you not know that, just as the foot spoke of if viewed apart will cease to be a foot, so you will cease to be a man? For what is a man? A part of a city, first a part of the City in which gods and men are incorporate, and secondly of that city which has the next claim to be called so, which is a small copy of the City universal.

'What,' you say, 'am I now to be put on my trial?'

Is another then to have a fever, another to go a voyage, another die, another be condemned? I say it is impossible in a body like ours, in this enveloping space, in this common life, that events of this sort should not happen, one to this man and another to that. It is your business then to take what fate brings and deal with what happens, as is fitting. Suppose then the judge says, 'I will judge you to be a wrongdoer'; you reply, 'May it go well with you! I did my part, and it is for you to see if you have done yours: for the judge's part too, do not forget, has its own danger!'

CHAPTER SIX

On what is Meant by 'Indifferent' Things

TAKE A GIVEN HYPOTHETICAL proposition. In itself it is indifferent, but your judgement upon it is not indifferent, but is either knowledge, or mere opinion, or delusion. In the same way though life is indifferent, the way you deal with it is not indifferent. Therefore, when you are told

'These things also are indifferent', do not be careless, and when you are urged to be careful, do not show a mean spirit and be overawed by material things.

It is a good thing to know what you can do and what you are prepared for, that in matters where you are not prepared, you may keep quiet and not be vexed if others have the advantage of you there. For when it is a question of syllogisms, you in your turn will expect to have the advantage, and if they are vexed with this you will console them with the words, 'I learnt them, but you did not. So when acquired dexterity is needed it is for you in your turn not to seek what only practice can give: leave that to those who have acquired the knack, and be content yourself to show constancy.

'Go and salute such an one.'

I have saluted him.

'How?'

In no mean spirit.

'But his house was shut upon you.'

Yes, for I have not learnt to enter by the window: when I find the door shut, I must either retire or go in by the window.

'But again one says, "Talk to him."'

I do talk to him.

'How?'

In no mean spirit.

Suppose you did not get what you wanted? Surely that was his business and not yours. Why then do you claim what is another's? If you always remember what is yours and what is not yours, you will never be put to confusion. Therefore Chrysippus well says, 'As long as the consequences are unknown to me, I always hold fast to what is better adapted to secure what is natural, for God Himself created me with the faculty of choosing what is natural.' Nay, if I really knew that it was ordained for me now to be ill, I should wish to be ill; for the foot too, if it had a mind, would wish to get muddy.

For instance, why do ears of corn grow? Is it not that they may ripen in the sun? And if they are ripened is it not that they may be reaped, for they are not things apart? If they had feelings then, ought they to pray never to be reaped at any time? But this is a curse upon corn–to pray that it should never be reaped. In like manner know that you are cursing men when you pray for them not to die: it is like a prayer not to be ripened, not to be reaped. But we men, being creatures whose fate it is to be reaped, are also made aware of this very fact, that we are destined for reaping, and so we are angry; for we do not know who we are, nor have we studied human things as those who are skilled in horses study the concerns of horses.

But Chrysantas, when he was about to strike the enemy, and heard the bugle sounding the retreat, desisted: so convinced was he that it was more to his advantage to do the general's bidding than his own. But not a man of us, even when necessity calls, is willing to obey her easily, but we bear what comes upon us with tears and groans, and we call it ‘circumstances’.

What do you mean by ‘circumstances’, fellow men? If you mean by ‘circumstances’ what surrounds you, everything is circumstance: if you use the term in the sense of hardships, how is it a hardship that what was born should be destroyed? The instrument of destruction is a sword or a wheel or the sea or a potsherd or a tyrant. What matters it to you, by what road you are to go down to Hades? All roads are alike. But, if you will hear the truth, the road the tyrant sends you is shorter. No tyrant ever took six months to execute a man, but a fever often takes a year to kill one. All these complaints are mere noise and vanity of idle phrases.

‘In Caesar’s presence my life is in danger.’

But am not I in equal danger, dwelling in Nicopolis, where earthquakes are so many? And you too, when you sail across the Adriatic, are you not in danger of your life?

'Yes, but in thought too I am in danger.'

Your thought? How can that be? Who can compel you to think against your will? The thought of others? How can it be any danger to you for others to have false ideas?

'Yes, but I am in danger of being banished.'

What is being banished? Is it being elsewhere than in Rome? 'Yes, suppose I am sent to Gyara?'

If it makes for your good, you will go: if not, you have a place to go to instead of Gyara, a place whither he who is sending you to Gyara will also go whether he will or no. Why then do you go to Rome as though it meant so much? It is not much compared with your preparation for it: so that a youth of fine feeling may say, 'It was not worth this price–to have heard so many lectures and written so many exercises, and sat at the feet of an old man of no great merit.'

There is only one thing for you to remember, that is, the distinction between what is yours and what is not yours.

Never lay claim to anything that is not your own. Tribunal and prison are distinct places, one high, the other low; but your will, if you choose to keep it the same in both, may be kept the same. So we shall emulate Socrates, but only when we can write songs of triumph in prison. As for our condition up till now, I doubt whether we should have borne with one who should say to us in prison, 'Would you like me to recite to you songs of triumph?'

'Why do you trouble me? Do you not know the ills which beset me? for this is my state.'

What is it?

'I am at the point of death.'

Yes, but are other men going to be immortal?

CHAPTER SEVEN

How to Consult Diviners

MANY OF US OFTEN neglect acts which are fitting because we consult the diviners out of season. What can the diviner see more than death or danger or disease or generally things of that sort? If then I have to risk my life for a friend, if even it is fitting for me to die for him, how can it be in season for me to consult a diviner? Have I not within me the diviner who has told me the true nature of good and evil, who has expounded the signs of both? What need have I then of the flesh of victims or the flight of birds? Can I bear with him when he says, 'This is expedient for you'? Does he know what is expedient, does he know what is good, has he learnt signs to distinguish between good things and bad, like the signs in the flesh of victims? If he knows the signs of good and evil, he knows also the signs of things noble and shameful, just and unjust. It is yours, man, to tell me what is portended–life or death, poverty or wealth; but whether this is expedient or inexpedient I am not going to inquire of you.

Why do you not lay down the law in matters of grammar? Are you going to do it here then, where all mankind are at sea and in conflict with one another? Therefore that was a good answer that the lady made who wished to send the shipload of supplies to Gratilla in exile, when one said, 'Domitian will take them away': 'I would rather', she said, 'that Domitian should take them away than that I should not send them.'

What then leads us to consult diviners so constantly? Cowardice, fear of events. That is why we flatter the diviners.

'Master, shall I inherit from my father?'

'Let us see: let us offer sacrifice.'

'Yes, master, as fortune wills.'

When he says, 'You shall inherit', we give thanks to him as though we had received the inheritance from him. That is why they go on deluding us.

What must we do then? We must come without the will to get or the will to avoid, just as the wayfarer asks the man he meets which of two ways leads anywhere, not wanting the right hand to be the road rather than the left, for he does not wish to go one particular road, but the road which leads to his goal. We ought to approach God as we approach a guide, dealing with Him as we deal with our eyes, not beseeching them to show us one sort of things rather than another, but accepting the impressions of things as they are shown us. But instead of that we tremble and get hold of the augur and appeal to him as if he were a god and say, 'Master, have pity, suffer me to come off safe.'

Slave, do you not wish for what is better for you? Is anything better than what seems good to God? Why do you do all that in you lies to corrupt the judge, and pervert your counsellor?

CHAPTER EIGHT

What is the True Nature of the Good

GOD IS BENEFICENT, but the good also is beneficent. It is natural therefore that the true nature of the good should be in the same region as the true nature of God. What then is the nature of God? Is it flesh? God forbid. Land? God forbid. Fame? God forbid. It is intelligence, knowledge, right reason. In these then and nowhere else seek the true nature of the good. Do you look for it in a plant? No. Or in an irrational creature? No. If then you seek it in what is rational why do you seek it elsewhere than in what distinguishes it from irrational things? Plants have not the faculty of dealing with impressions; therefore you do not predicate 'good' of them.

The good then demands power to deal with impressions. Is that all it demands? If that be all, you must say that other animals also are capable of good and of happiness and unhappiness. But you do not say so and you are right, for whatever power they may have to deal with impressions, they have not the power to understand how they do so, and with good reason, for they are subservient to others, and are not of primary importance.

Take the ass, for instance, is it born to be of primary importance? No; it is born because we had need of a back able to bear burdens.

Nay, more, we had need that it should walk; therefore it has further received the power of dealing with impressions, for else it could not have walked. Beyond that its powers cease. But if the ass itself had received the power to understand how it deals with impressions, then it is plain that reason would have required that it should not have been subject to us or have supplied these needs, but should have been our equal and like ourselves. Will you not then seek the true nature of the good in that, the want of which makes you refuse to predicate good of other things?

'What do you mean? Are not they too God's works?'

They are, but not His principal works, nor parts of the Divine. But you are a principal work, a fragment of God Himself, you have in yourself a part of Him. Why then are you ignorant of your high birth? Why do you not know whence you have come? Will you not remember, when you eat, who you are that eat, and whom you are feeding, and the same in your relations with women? When you take part in society, or training, or conversation, do you not know that it is God you are nourishing and training? You bear God about with you, poor wretch, and know it not. Do you think I speak of some external god of silver or gold? No, you bear Him about within you and are unaware that you are defiling Him with unclean thoughts and foul actions. If an image of God were present, you would not dare to do any of the things you do; yet when God Himself is present within you and sees and hears all things, you are not ashamed of thinking and acting thus: O slow to understand your nature, and estranged from God!

Again, when we send a young man from school to the world of action, why is it that we fear that he may do something amiss– in eating, in relations with women, that he may be humbled by wearing rags, or puffed up by fine clothes?

He does not know the God that is in him,

he knows not in whose company he is going. Can we allow him to say, 'I would fain have you with me'? Have you not God there? and, having Him, do you look for any one else? Will He tell you anything different from this? Why, if you were a statue wrought by Phidias–his Zeus or his Athena–you would have remembered what you are and the Craftsman who made you, and if you had any intelligence, you would have tried to do nothing unworthy of him who made you or of yourself, and to bear yourself becomingly in men's eyes. But as it is, do you, whom Zeus has made, for that reason take no thought what manner of man you will show yourself? Yet what comparison is there between the one artificer and the other or the one work and the other? What work of art, for instance, has in itself the faculties of which it gives indication in its structure? Is it not stone or bronze or gold or ivory? Even the Athena of Phidias having once for all stretched out her hand and received the Victory upon it stands thus for all time, but the works of God are endowed with movement and breath, and have the faculty of dealing with impressions and of testing them.

When this Craftsman has made you, do you dishonour his work? Nay, more, He not only made you, but committed you as a trust to yourself and none other. Will you not remember this, but even dishonour the trust committed to you?

If God had committed some orphan to your care, would you have neglected him so? Yet He has entrusted your own self to you and He says, 'I had none other more trustworthy than you: keep this man for me such as he is born to be, modest, faithful, high-minded, undismayed, free from passion and tumult.' After that, do you refuse to keep him so?

But they will say, 'Where has this man got his high looks and his lofty countenance?'

Nay, I have not got them yet as I ought: for as yet I have not confidence in what I have learnt and assented to, I still fear my own weakness. Only let me gain confidence and then you shall see a proper aspect and a proper bearing, then I will show you the statue as it is when it is finished and polished. What think you? That this means proud looks? Heaven forbid! Does Zeus of Olympia wear proud looks? No, but his gaze is steadfast, as his should be who is to say:

For my word cannot be taken back, nor can it deceive.

[Homer, **Iliad**, I. 256]

Such will I show myself to you–faithful, self-respecting, noble, free from tumult.

'Do you mean, free from death and old age and disease?'

No, but as one who dies as a god, and who bears illness like a god. These are my possessions, these my faculties; all others are beyond me. I will show you the sinews of a philosopher.

'What do you mean by sinews?'

Will to achieve that fails not, will to avoid

that falls not into evil, impulse to act appropriately, strenuous purpose, assent that is not precipitate. This is what you shall see.

CHAPTER NINE

That we Adopt the Profession of the Philosopher when we cannot Fulfil that of a Man

IT IS NO ORDINARY task merely to fulfil man's promise. For what is Man? A rational animal, subject to death. At once we ask, from what does the rational element distinguish us? From wild beasts. And from what else?

From sheep and the like. Look to it then that you do nothing like a wild beast, else you destroy the Man in you and fail to fulfil his promise. See that you do not act like a sheep, or else again the Man in you perishes.

You ask how we act like sheep?

When we consult the belly, or our passions, when our actions are random or dirty or inconsiderate, are we not falling away to the state of sheep? What do we destroy? The faculty of reason. When our actions are combative, mischievous, angry, and rude, do we not fall away and become wild beasts? In a word, some of us are great beasts, and others are small but base-natured beasts, which give occasion to say, 'Nay, rather let me be food for a lion.' All these are actions by which the calling of man is destroyed.

What makes a complex proposition be what it is? It must fulfil its promise: it keeps its character only if the parts it is composed of are true. What makes a disjunctive proposition? It must fulfil its purport. Is not the same true of flutes, lyre, horse, and dog? Is it surprising then that man too keeps or loses his nature on the same principle? Each man is strengthened and preserved by the exercise of the functions that correspond to his nature, the carpenter by carpentering, the grammarian by studies in grammar. If a man gets the habit of writing ungrammatically, his art is bound to be destroyed and perish. In the same way the modest man is made by modest acts and ruined by immodest acts, the man of honour keeps his character by honest acts and loses it by dishonest. So again men of the opposite character are strengthened by the opposite actions: the shameless man by shamelessness, the dishonest by dishonesty, the slanderous by slander, the ill-tempered by ill-temper, the miser by grasping at more than he gives. That is why philosophers enjoin upon us 'not to be content with learning only, but to add practice as well and then training'. For we have acquired wrong habits in course of years and have adopted for our use conceptions opposite to the true, and therefore if we do not adopt true conceptions for our use we shall be nothing else but interpreters of judgements which are not our own.

Of course any one of us can discourse for the moment on what is good and what is bad: as thus, 'Of things that are, some are good, some bad, some indifferent; good are virtues and things that have part in virtues; evil are the opposite; indifferent are wealth, health, reputation.' And then if some loud noise disturbs us while we are speaking or one of the bystanders laughs at us, we are put out of countenance. Philosopher, where are those principles you were talking of? Whence did you fetch them forth to utter? From the lips and no further.

These principles are not your own: why do you make a mess of them? Why do you gamble with things of highest moment? It is one thing (to use an illustration) to put bread and wine away into a store-cupboard, and another thing to eat. What you eat is digested and distributed, and is turned into sinews, flesh, bones, blood, complexion, breath. What you store away you have at hand and can show to others at will, but it does you no good except for the mere name of having it. What is the good of expounding these doctrines any more than those of another school? Sit down now and discourse on the doctrines of Epicurus, and you will soon discourse more effectively than Epicurus himself. Why then do you call yourself a Stoic, why do you deceive the world, why being a Hellene do you act the Jew? Do you not see in what sense a man is called a Jew, in what sense a Syrian, in what an Egyptian? When we see a man trimming between two faiths we are wont to say, 'He is no Jew, but is acting a part', but when he adopts the attitude of mind of him who is baptized and has made his choice, then he is not only called a Jew but is a Jew indeed. So we also are but counterfeit 'baptists',

Jews in name only, but really something else, with no feeling for reason, far from acting on the principles we talk of, though we pride ourselves on them as though we knew them. So, being unable to fulfil the calling of Man we adopt that of the Philosopher, a heavy burden indeed! It is as though one who could not lift ten pounds were fain to lift the stone of Ajax!

CHAPTER TEN

How the Acts Appropriate to Man are to be Discovered from the Names he Bears

CONSIDER WHO YOU ARE. First, a Man; that is, one who has nothing more sovereign than will, but all else subject to this, and will itself free from slavery or subjection. Consider then from what you are parted by reason. You are parted from wild beasts, you are parted from sheep. On these terms you are a citizen of the universe and a part of it, not one of those marked for service, but of those fitted for command; for you have the faculty to understand the divine governance of the universe and to reason on its sequence. What then is the calling of a Citizen? To have no personal interest, never to think about anything as though he were detached, but to be like the hand or the foot, which, if they had the power of reason and understood the order of nature, would direct every impulse and every process of the will by reference to the whole. That is why it is well said by philosophers that 'if the good man knew coming events beforehand he would help on nature, even if it meant working with disease, and death and maiming', for he would realize that by the ordering of the universe this task is allotted him, and that the whole is more commanding than the part and the city than the citizen. 'But seeing that we do not know beforehand, it is appropriate that we should hold fast to the things that are by nature more fit to be chosen; for indeed we are born for this.'

Next remember that you are a Son. What part do we expect a son to play? His part is to count all that is his as his father's, to obey him in all things, never to speak ill of him to any, nor to say or do anything to harm him, to give way to him and yield him place in all things, working with him so far as his powers allow.

Next know that you are also a Brother. For this part too you are bound to show a spirit of concession and obedience; and to speak kindly, and not to claim against another anything that is outside the will, but gladly to sacrifice those things, that you may gain in the region where your will has control. For look what a thing it is to gain good nature at the price of a lettuce, if it so chance, or the surrender of a chair:

what a gain is that!

Next, if you are a member of a city council, remember that you are a councillor; if young, that you are young; if old, that you are old; if a father, that you are a father. For each of these names, if properly considered, suggests the acts appropriate to it. But if you go and disparage your brother, I tell you that you are forgetting who you are and what is your name. I say, if you were a smith and used your hammer wrong, you would have forgotten the smith; but if you forget the brother's part and turn into an enemy instead of a brother, are you going to imagine that you have undergone no change? If instead of man, a gentle and sociable creature, you have become a dangerous, aggressive, and biting brute, have you lost nothing? Do you think you must lose cash in order to suffer damage? Does no other sort of loss damage man? If you lost skill in grammar or music you would count the loss as damage; if you are going to lose honour and dignity and gentleness, do you count it as nothing? Surely those other losses are due to some external cause outside our will, but these are due to ourselves. Those qualities it is no honour to have and no dishonour to lose, but these you cannot lack or lose without dishonour, reproach, and disaster.

What does he lose who is the victim of unnatural lust? He loses his manhood. And the agent of such lust, what does he lose? He loses his manhood like the other, and much besides. What does the adulterer lose? He loses the man of honour and self-control, the gentleman, the citizen, the neighbour. What does the angry man lose? Something else. The man who fears? Something else. No one is evil without destruction and loss.

If on the other hand you look for loss in paltry pence, all the men I have mentioned are without loss or damage, if it so chance, nay they actually receive gain and profit, when they get cash by any of these actions. But notice, that if you make money the standard in everything, you will not count even the man who loses his nose as having suffered injury.

'Yes, I do,' he says, 'for his body is mutilated.'

Well, but does the man who has lost, not his nose but his sense of smell, lose nothing? Is there no faculty of the mind, which brings gain to him that gets it and hurt to him that loses it?

'What can possibly be the faculty you mean?'

Have we no natural sense of honour?

'We have.'

Does he that destroys this suffer no damage, no deprivation, no loss of what belongs to him? Have we not a natural faculty of trust, a natural gift of affection, of beneficence, of mutual toleration? Are we then to count the man who suffers himself to be injured in regard to these as free from loss and damage?

'What conclusion do you draw? Am I not to harm him who harmed me?'

First consider what 'harm' means and remember what you heard from the philosophers. For if good lies in the will and evil also lies in the will, look whether what you are saying does not come to this: 'What do you mean? As he harmed himself by doing me a wrong, am I not to harm myself by doing him a wrong?' Why then do we not look at things in this light? When we suffer some loss in body or property, we count it hurt: is there no hurt, when we suffer loss in respect of our will?

Of course the man who is deceived or the man who does a wrong has no pain in his head or his eye or his hip, nor does he lose his estate; and these are the things we care for, nothing else. But we take no concern whatever whether our will is going to be kept honourable and trustworthy or shameless and faithless, except only so far as we discuss it in the lecture-room, and therefore so far as our wretched discussions go we make some progress, but beyond them not the least.

CHAPTER ELEVEN

What is the Beginning of Philosophy

THE BEGINNING OF PHILOSOPHY with those who approach it in the right way and by the door is a consciousness of one's own weakness and want of power in regard to necessary things. For we come into the world with no innate conception of a right-angled triangle, or of a quarter-tone or of a semi-tone, but we are taught what each of these means by systematic instruction; and therefore those who are ignorant of these things do not think that they know them. On the other hand every one has come into the world with an innate conception as to good and bad, noble and shameful, becoming and unbecoming, happiness and unhappiness, fitting and inappropriate, what is right to do and what is wrong. Therefore we all use these terms and try to fit our preconceived notions to particular facts. 'He did nobly', 'dutifully', 'un-dutifully'. 'He was unfortunate', 'he was fortunate'; 'he is unjust', 'he is just.' Which of us refrains from these phrases? Which of us puts off using them until he is taught them, just as men who have no knowledge of lines or sounds refrain from talking of them? The reason is that on the subject in question we come into the world with a certain amount of teaching, so to say, already given us by nature; to this basis of knowledge we have added our own fancies.

'Why!' says he; 'do I not know what is noble and what is shameful? Have I no conception of them?'

You have.

'Do I not fit my conception to particulars?'

You do.

'Do I not fit them well then?'

There lies the whole question and there fancy comes in. For, starting with these admitted principles, men advance to the matter in dispute, applying these principles inappropriately. For if they really possessed this faculty as well, what would prevent them from being perfect? You think that you apply your preconceptions properly to particular cases; but tell me, how do you arrive at this?

I have such a conviction.

But another has a different conviction, has he not, and yet believes. as you do, that he is applying his conception rightly?

He does.

Is it possible then for you both to apply your conceptions properly in matters on which you hold contrary opinion?

It is impossible.

Can you then point us to anything beyond your own opinion which will enable us to apply our conceptions better? Does the madman do anything else but what he thinks right? Is this criterion then sufficient for him too?

It is not.

Come, then, let us look for something beyond personal opinion. Where shall we find it?

Here you see the beginning of philosophy, in the discovery of the conflict of men's minds with one another, and the attempt to seek for the reason of this conflict, and the condemnation of mere opinion, as a thing not to be trusted; and a search to determine whether your opinion is true, and an attempt to discover a standard, just as we discover the balance to deal with weights and the rule to deal with things straight and crooked. This is the beginning of philosophy.

'Are all opinions right which all men hold?'

Nay, how is it possible for contraries to be both right?

'Well, then, not all opinions, but our opinions?'

Why ours, rather than those of the Syrians or the Egyptians, or the personal opinion of myself or of this man or that?

'Why indeed?'

So then, what each man thinks is not sufficient to make a thing so: for in dealing with weights and measures we are not satisfied with mere appearance, but have found a standard to determine each. Is there, then, no standard here beyond opinion? It is impossible surely that things most necessary among men should be beyond discovery and beyond proof?

There is a standard then. Then, why do we not seek it and find it, and having found it use it hereafter without fail, never so much as 'stretching out our finger' without it? For it is this standard, I suppose, the discovery of which relieves from madness those who wrongly use personal opinion as their only measure, and enables us thereafter to start from known principles, clearly defined, and so to apply our conceptions to particulars in definite and articulate form.

What subject, I might ask, lies before us for our present discussion? 'Pleasure.'

Submit it to the rule, put it in the balance. Ought the good to be something which is worthy to inspire confidence and trust? 'It ought.'

Is it proper to have confidence in anything which is insecure? 'No.'

Has pleasure, then, any certainty in it?

'No.'

Away with it then! Cast it from the scales and drive it far away from the region of good things. But if your sight is not keen, and you are not satisfied with one set of scales, try another.

Is it proper to be elated at what is good?

'It is.'

Is it proper, then, to be elated at the pleasure of the moment? Be careful how you say that it is proper. If you do, I shall not count you worthy of the scales.

Thus things are judged and weighed if we have standards ready to test them: and in fact the work of philosophy is to investigate and firmly establish such standards; and the duty of the good man is to proceed to apply the decisions arrived at.

CHAPTER TWELVE

On the Art of Discussion

OUR PHILOSOPHERS HAVE PRECISELY defined what a man must learn in order to know how to argue: but we are still quite unpractised in the proper use of what we have learnt. Give any one of us you like an unskilled person to argue with, and he does not discover how to deal with him: he just rouses the man for a moment, and then if he answers him in the wrong key he cannot deal with him any longer: he either reviles him or laughs at him ever after, and says, 'He is an ignoramus, there is nothing to be got out of him.'

But the true guide, when he finds a man wandering, leads him to the right road, instead of leaving him with a gibe or an insult. So should you do. Only show him the truth and you will see that he follows. But so long as you do not show it him, do not laugh at him, but rather realize your own incapacity.

Now how did Socrates proceed? He compelled the man who was conversing with him to be his witness, and needed no witness besides. Therefore he was able to say: 'I am satisfied with my opponent as a witness, and let every one else alone: and I do not take the votes of other people, but only of him who is arguing with me.' [Plato, **Gorgias**, 474a] For he drew out so clearly the consequences of a man's conceptions that every one realized the contradiction and abandoned it.

'Does the man who envies rejoice in his envy?'

'Not at all; he is pained rather than pleased.'

Thus he rouses his neighbour by contradiction.

'Well, does envy seem to you to be a feeling of pain at evil things? Yet how can there be envy of things evil?'

So he makes his opponent say that envy is pain felt at good things. 'Again, can a man envy things which do not concern him?' 'Certainly not.'

In this way he made the conception full and articulate, and so went away. He did not say, 'Define me envy', and then, when the man defined it, 'You define it ill, for the terms of the definition do not correspond to the subject defined.' Such phrases are technical and therefore tiresome to the lay mind, and hard to follow, yet you and I cannot get away from them. We are quite unable to rouse the ordinary man's attention in a way which will enable him to follow his own impressions and so arrive at admitting or rejecting this or that. And therefore those of us who are at all cautious naturally give the subject up, when we become aware of this incapacity; while the mass of men, who venture at random into this sort of enterprise, muddle others and get muddled themselves, and end by abusing their opponents and getting abused in return, and so leave the field. But the first quality of all in Socrates, and the most characteristic, was that he never lost his temper in argument, never uttered anything abusive, never anything insolent, but bore with abuse from others and quieted strife. If you would get to know what a faculty he had in this matter, read the Banquet of Xenophon and you will see how many strifes he has brought to an end. Therefore the poets too with good reason have praised this gift most highly:

And straightway with skill he brought to rest a mighty quarrel.

[Hesiod, **Theogony**, 87]

What follows? The occupation is not a very safe one nowadays, and especially in Rome. For he who pursues it will certainly not have to do it in a corner, but he must go up to a consular or a rich man, if it so chance, and ask him: 'You there, can you tell me to whose care you trust your horses?'

'Yes.'

Do you trust them to a chance corner and one unskilled in horse-keeping?

'Certainly not.'

Again, tell me to whom you trust your gold or your silver or your clothes.

'Not to a chance corner either.'

And your body–have you ever thought of trusting that to anybody to look after it?

'Certainly.'

He too, no doubt, is one skilled in the art of training or of medicine, is he not?

'Certainly he is.'

Are these then your best possessions or have you got something besides, better than all?

'What can you mean?'

I mean, of course, that which makes use of all these possessions and tests each one, and thinks about them.

'Do you mean the soul?'

You are right; that is exactly what I do mean.

'Yes, I certainly think that this is a better possession than all the rest.'

Can you tell me, then, in what manner you have taken care of your soul? for it is not likely that one so wise as you. and of such position in the state, should lightly and recklessly allow the best possession you have to be neglected and go to ruin.

'Certainly not.'

Well, have you taken care of it yourself? Did any one teach you how, or did you find out for yourself?

When you do this, the danger is, you will find, that first he will say: 'My good sir, what concern is it of yours? Are you my master?' Then, if you persist in annoying him he will lift his hand and give you a drubbing.

That (says Epictetus) was a pursuit I had a keen taste for once, before I was reduced to my present condition.

CHAPTER THIRTEEN

Concerning Anxiety

WHEN I SEE A man in a state of anxiety, I say, 'What can this man want? If he did not want something which is not in his power, how could he still be anxious? It is for this reason that one who sings to the lyre is not anxious when he is performing by himself, but when he enters the theatre, even if he has a very good voice and plays well: for he not only wants to perform well, but also to win a great name, and that is beyond his own control.

In fact, where he has knowledge there he has confidence. Bring in any unskilled person you like, and he pays no heed to him. On the other hand he is anxious whenever he has no knowledge and has made no study of the subject. What does this mean? He does not know what 'the people' is, nor what its praise is worth: he has learnt to strike the bottom note or the top note, but he does not know what the praise of the multitude is, nor what value it has in life; he has made no study of that. So he is bound to tremble and grow pale.

When I see a man, then, in this state of fear I cannot say that he is no performer with the lyre, but I can say something else of him, and not one thing but many. And first of all I call him a stranger and say, This man does not know where in the world he is; though he has been with us so long, he does not know the laws and customs of the City–what he may do and what he may not do–no, nor has he called in a lawyer at any time to tell him and explain to him what are the requirements of the law. Of course he does not draw up a will without knowing how he ought to draw it up, or without calling in one who knows, nor does he lightly put his seal to a guarantee or give a written security; but he calls in no lawyer when he is exercising the will to get and will to avoid, impulse and intention and purpose. What do I mean by 'having no lawyer'? I mean that he does not know that he is wishing to have what is not given him, and wishing not to have what he cannot avoid, and he does not know what is his own and what is not his own. If he did know, he would never feel hindrance or constraint or anxiety; how could he? Does any one fear about things which are not evil?

'No.'

Or again about things which are evil but are in his power to prevent? 'Certainly not.'

If, then, nothing beyond our will's control is

either good or evil, and everything within our will's control depends entirely on ourselves, so that no one can take any such thing away from us or win it for us against our will, what room is left for anxiety? Yet we are anxious for our bit of a body, for our bit of property, for what Caesar will think, but are not anxious at all for what is within us. Am I anxious about not conceiving a false thought? No, for that depends on myself.

Or about indulging an impulse contrary to nature?

No, not about this either. So, when you see a man pale, just as the physician, judging from his colour, says, 'This man's spleen is out of order, or that man's liver', so do you say, 'This man is disordered in the will to get and the will to avoid, he is not in the right way, he is feverish'; for nothing else changes the complexion and causes a man to tremble and his teeth to chatter,

and droop the knee and sink upon his feet.

[Homer, **Iliad**, XIII, 281]

Therefore Zeno was not distressed when he was going to meet Antigonus, for Antigonus had no authority over any of the things that Zeno admired, and Zeno paid no attention to the possessions of Antigonus. Antigonus was anxious when he was going to meet Zeno, and with good reason, for he wanted to please him, and this lay beyond his control; but Zeno did not wish to please Antigonus, any more than any artist cares to please one who has no skill.

Do I want to please you? Why should I? Do you know the standards by which man judges man? Have you made it your study to learn what a good man is and what a bad man is, and what makes each of them so? Why, then, are you not good yourself?

'Not good? What do you mean?' he replies.

Why, no good man whines or groans

or laments, no good man grows pale or trembles or says, 'How will he receive me? What hearing will he give me?'

Slave, he will do as he thinks good. What concern have you in what does not belong to you? Is it not his fault if he gives a bad reception to what you offer?

'His fault, certainly.'

But can the fault be one man's and the harm another's?

'No.'

Why, then, are you anxious about another's concerns?

'Nay, but I am anxious to know how I am to address him.' What, is it not in your power to address him as you will? 'Yes, but I am afraid I may lose my self-possession.'

Are you afraid of losing your self-possession when you are going to write the name Dion?

'Certainly not.'

What is the reason? Is it not, that you have practised writing?

Of course it is. Or again, when you are about to read, would you not be in like case?

'Exactly.'

What is the reason? The reason is that every art contains within it an element of strength and confidence. Have you not practised speaking, then? What else did you study at school? You studied syllogisms and variable arguments. What for? Was it not that .you might converse with skill, and does not 'with skill' mean in good season, with security and good sense, and, more than that, without failure or hindrance, and, to crown all, with confidence?

'Yes.'

Well, if you are a rider and have to confront a man on foot in the plain, where you have the advantage of practice and he has not, are you anxious?

'Nay, but he has power to put me to death.'

Miserable man, tell the truth and be not a braggart nor claim to be a philosopher. Know who are your masters. As long as you give them this hold over your body, you must follow every one who is stronger than you.

But Socrates, who spoke to the Tyrants, to his judges, and in prison, in the tone we know, had studied speaking to some purpose. So had Diogenes, who spoke in the same tone to Alexander, to Philip, to the pirates, to his purchaser. . . . Leave this to those who have made it their concern, to the confident: and do you go to your own concerns and never leave them again. Go and sit in your corner and weave syllogisms and propound them to others,

No ruler of a state is found in you.

[Author unknown]

CHAPTER FOURTEEN

On Naso

ONCE WHEN A ROMAN came in with his son and was listening to one of his lectures Epictetus said: 'This is the method of my teaching', and broke off short. And when the Roman begged him to continue, he replied:–Every art, when it is being taught, is tiresome to one who is unskilled and untried in it. The products of the arts indeed show at once the use they are made for, and most of them have an attraction and charm of their own; for though it is no pleasure to be present and follow the process by which a shoemaker learns his art, the shoe itself is useful and a pleasant thing to look at as well. So too the process by which a carpenter learns is very tiresome to the unskilled person who happens to be by, but his work shows the use of his art. This you will see still more in the case of music, for if you are by when a man is being taught you will think the process of all things the most unpleasant, yet the effects of music are pleasant and delightful for unmusical persons to hear.

So with philosophy; we picture to ourselves the work of the philosopher to be something of this sort: he must bring his own will into harmony with events, in such manner that nothing which happens should happen against our will, and that we should not wish for anything to happen that does not happen. The result of this is that those who have thus ordered their life do not fail to get what they will, and do not fall into what they will to avoid: each man spends his own life free from pain, from fear, and from distraction, and maintains the natural and acquired relations which unite him to his fellows–the part of son, father, brother, citizen, husband, wife, neighbour, fellow traveller, ruler, subject.

Such is the business of the philosopher as we picture it. The next thing is that we seek how we are to achieve it. Now we see that the carpenter becomes a carpenter by learning certain things, the helmsman becomes a helmsman by learning certain things. May we, then, infer that in the sphere of conduct too it is not enough merely to wish to become good, but one must learn certain things? We have, then, to look and see what these things are. The philosophers say that the first thing one must learn is this: 'that God exists and provides for the universe, and it is impossible for a man to act or even to conceive a thought or reflection without God knowing. The next thing is to learn the true nature of the gods. For whatever their nature is discovered to be, he that is to please and obey them must needs try, so far as he can, to make himself like them.' If God is faithful, he must be faithful too; if free, he must be free too; if beneficent, he too must be beneficent: if high-minded, he must be high-minded: he must, in fact, as one who makes God his ideal, follow this out in every act and word.

'At what point, then, must we begin?'

If you attempt this task, I will tell you, that you must first understand terms.

'What? Do you imply that I do not understand terms now?' You do not.

'How then do I use them?'

You use them as illiterate persons deal with written sounds, as cattle deal with impressions: for it is one thing to use them, and another to understand. If you think you understand them, let us take any term you like and put ourselves to the test, to see if we understand.

'But it is vexatious when one is getting old, and has served, if it so chance, one's three campaigns, to be put through an examination.'

I know that as well as you. You have come to me now as if you were in want of nothing: and indeed what could you be imagined as wanting? You are rich, you have children, it may be, and a wife and many servants, the Emperor knows you, you possess many friends in Rome, you perform the acts appropriate to you, you know how to return good for good and evil for evil. What do you lack? If I show you that you lack what is most necessary and important for happiness, and that hitherto you have paid attention to everything rather than to acting appropriately, and if I conclude my criticism by saying that you do not know what God or man is, or what good or evil is, though perhaps you may bear being told of your ignorance in other ways, you cannot bear with me when I say that you do not know your own self; how can you submit to examination and abide my question? You cannot bear it at all: you go away at once in disgust. And yet what evil have I done you? Unless indeed the mirror does harm to the ugly man, by showing him what sort of man he is: unless the physician too insults the sick man, when he says to him, 'Sir, you think there is nothing wrong with you, but you are in a fever; take no food to-day and drink water'; and no one says, 'What shocking insolence!' But if you say to a man, 'There is fever in your will to get, your will to avoid is degraded, your designs are inconsistent, your impulses out of harmony with nature, your conceptions random and false', he goes away at once and says, 'He insulted me!'

Our condition may be compared to the gathering at a public festival. Cattle and oxen are brought thither for sale, and the mass of men come to buy or to sell; only some few come to look at the assembled people

CHAPTER FIFTEEN

On those who Cling Stubbornly to their Judgements

THERE ARE SOME WHO when they hear these precepts–that a man must be steadfast, and that the will is by nature a free thing and not subject to compulsion, whereas all else is subject to hindrance and compulsion, being in bondage and dependence–imagine that they must abide without swerving by every judgement that they have formed. No–first of all the judgement arrived at must be sound.

For I would have the body firmly braced, but it must be the firmness of health and good condition; if you show me that you have the firmness of a madman and boast of that, I shall say to you, 'Look, man, for some one to cure you.' This is not firmness, but the opposite.

Let me describe another state of mind to be found in those who hear these precepts amiss. A friend of mine, for instance, determined for no reason to starve himself. I learnt of it when he was in the third day of his fasting, and went and asked him what had happened.

'I have decided', said he.

Yes, but, for all that, say what it was that persuaded you; for if your decision was right, here we are at your side ready to help you to leave this life, but, if your decision was against reason, then change your mind.

'A man must abide by his decisions.'

What are you doing, man? Not all decisions, but right decisions. For instance, if you were convinced at the moment that it was right, abide by that opinion if you think fit, and do not change it, but say, 'one must abide by one's decisions.'

Will you not lay this foundation to begin with–that is, examine your decision and see whether it is sound or unsound, and then afterwards build on it your firmness and unshaken resolve? But if you lay a rotten and crumbling foundation you will not be able to build even a tiny building; the more courses and the stronger that you lay upon it the quicker will it collapse. You are removing from life without any reason our familiar friend, our fellow citizen in the great City and the small, and then, though you are guilty of murder and of killing one who has done no wrong, you say, 'I must abide by my decisions.' If perchance it occurred to you to kill me, would you be bound to abide by your decisions?

Well, I had much ado to persuade that friend to change his mind. But it is impossible to move some of the men of to-day, so that I think that I know now what I did not know before, the meaning of the familiar saying, 'A fool is not to be persuaded nor broken of his folly.' May it never be my lot to have for friend a wise fool: nothing is more difficult to handle.

'I have decided.'

So have the madmen, but the more firmly they persist in false judgements the more hellebore do they require. Will you not act as the sick man should, and call in the physician? As he says, 'I am sick, master; help me: consider what I ought to do, it is for me to obey you', so you should say, 'I do not know what I ought to do, but I have come to learn.' Oh no, you say: 'Talk to me about other things; this I have decided.' Other things indeed! What is greater or more to your advantage than that you should be convinced that it is not sufficient to have decided and to refuse all change of mind? This is the firmness of madness, not of health.

'If you force me to this, I would fain die.'

Why, man, what has happened?

'I have decided.'

Lucky for me that you have not decided to kill me.

'I do not take fees.'

Why?

'I have decided.'

Let me tell you that the same energy with which you now refuse to take fees may incline you one day (what is to prevent it?) to take them and to say again, 'I have decided.'

Just as in an ailing body, which suffers from a flux, the flux inclines now to this part and now to that, so it is with a weak mind: no one can tell which way it sways, but when this swaying and drift has energy to back it, then the mischief becomes past help and remedy.

CHAPTER SIXTEEN

That we do not Practise Applying our Judgements About Things Good and Evil

WHERE LIES THE GOOD?

In a man's will.

Where lies evil?

In the will.

Where is the neutral sphere?

In the region outside the will's control.

Well, now, does any one of us remember these principles outside the lecture-room? Does any man practise by himself to answer facts as he would answer questions? For instance, is it day? 'Yes.' Again, is it night? 'No.' Again, are the stars even in number? 'I cannot say.' When money is shown you have you practised giving the proper answer, that it is not a good thing? Have you trained yourself in answers like this, or only to meet fallacious arguments? Why are you surprised, then, that you surpass yourself in the sphere where you have practised, and make no progress where you are unpractised?

Why is it that the orator, though he knows that he has written a good speech, and has got by heart what he has written, and brings a pleasant voice to his task, still feels anxiety in spite of all? The reason is that merely to declaim his speech does not content him. What does he want then? To be praised by his audience. Now he has been trained to be able to declaim, but he has not been trained in regard to praise and blame. For when did he hear from any one what praise is and what blame is: what is the nature of each, what manner of praise must be pursued, and what manner of blame must be avoided? When did he go through this training in accordance with these principles?

Why, then, are you still surprised that he is superior to others in the things he has been taught, and on a level with the mass of men in the things he has not studied? He is like the singer accompanying the lyre who knows how to play, sings well, and wears a fine tunic, and yet trembles when he comes on; for though he has all this knowledge he does not know what the people is or the clamour or mockery of the people. Nay, he does not even know what this anxiety is that he is feeling, whether it depends on himself or on another, whether it can be suppressed or not. Therefore, if men praise him, he leaves the stage puffed up; if they mock him, his poor bubble of conceit is pricked and subsides.

Very much the same is our position. What do we admire? External things. What are we anxious about? External things. And yet we are at a loss to know how fears or anxiety assail us! What else can possibly happen when we count impending events as evil? We cannot be free from fear, we cannot be free from anxiety. Yet we say, 'O Lord God, how am I to be rid of anxiety?' Fool, have you no hands? Did not God make them for you? Sit still and pray forsooth, that your rheum may not flow. Nay, wipe your nose rather and do not accuse God.

What moral do I draw? Has not God given you anything in the sphere of conduct? Has He not given you endurance, has He not given you greatness of mind, has He not given you manliness? When you have these strong hands to help you, do you still seek for one to wipe your rheum away?

But we do not practise such conduct nor pay attention to it. Find me one man who cares how he is going to do a thing, who is interested not in getting something but in realizing his true nature. Who is there that when walking is interested in his own activity, or when deliberating is interested in the act of deliberation, and not in getting that for which he is planning? And then if he succeeds he is elated and says, 'What a fine plan that was of ours! Did not I tell you, my brother, that if we have thought a thing out it is bound to happen so?' But if he fails he is humbled and miserable, and cannot find anything to say about what has happened. Which of us ever called in a prophet in order to realize his true nature? Which of us ever slept in a temple of dreams for this? Name the man. Give me but one, that I may set eyes on him I have long been seeking for, the man who is truly noble and has fine feeling; be he young or old, give me one.

Why, then, do we wonder any more that, whereas we are quite at home in dealing with material things, when we come to express ourselves in action we behave basely and unseemly, are worthless, cowardly, unenduring, failures altogether? But if we kept our fear not for death or exile, but for fear itself, then we should practise to avoid what we think evil. As it is we are glib and fluent in the lecture-room, and if any paltry question arises about a point of conduct, we are capable of pursuing the subject logically; but put us to the practical test and you will find us miserable shipwrecks. Let a distracting thought occur to us and you will soon find out for what we were studying and training. The result of our want of practice is that we are always heaping up terrors and imagining things bigger than they really are. When I go a voyage, as soon as I gaze down into the deep or look round on the sea and find no land, I am beside myself, imagining that if I am wrecked I must swallow all this sea, for it never occurs to me that three quarts are enough for me. What is it alarms me?

The sea? No, but my judgement about it. Again, when an earthquake happens, I imagine that the city is going to fall on me. What! Is not a tiny stone enough to knock my brains out?

What, then, are the burdens that weigh upon us and drive us out of our minds? What else but our judgements? When a man goes away and leaves the companions and the places and the society that he is used to, what else is it that weighs upon him but judgement? Children, when they cry a little because their nurse has left them, forget her as soon as they are given a bit of cake.

'Do you want us to be like children too?'

No, not at all; it is not by cake I would have you influenced, but by true judgements. What do I mean? I mean the judgements that a man must study all day long, uninfluenced by anything that does not concern him, whether it be companion or place or gymnasia, or even his own body; he must remember the law and keep this before his eyes.

What is the law of God?

To guard what is your own, not to claim what is another's; to use what is given you, not to long for anything if it be not given; if anything be taken away, to give it up at once and without a struggle, with gratitude for the time you have enjoyed it, if you would not cry for your nurse and your mammy. For what difference does it make what a man is a slave to, and what he depends on? How are you better than one who weeps for a mistress, if you break your heart for a paltry gymnasium and paltry colonnades and precious young men and that sort of occupation? Here comes a man complaining that he is not to drink the water of Dirce any more.

What! is not the Marcian water as good as that of Dirce?

'Nay, but I was used to the other.'

Yes, and you will get used to this in turn. I say, if such things are going to influence you, go away and cry for it, and try to write a line like that of Euripides,

The baths of Nero and the Marcian spring
[This line parodies Euripides,
The Phoenissae]

See how tragedy arises when fools have to face everyday events!

'When shall I see Athens again, then, and the Acropolis?'

Unhappy man, are you not content with what you see day by day? Can you set eyes on anything better or greater than the sun, the moon, the stars, the whole earth, the ocean? And if you really understand Him that governs the universe and if you carry Him about within you, do you still long for paltry stones and pretty rock? What will you do, then, when you are going to leave the very sun and moon? Shall you sit crying like little children? What were you doing, then, at school? What did you hear? What did you learn? Why did you write yourself down a philosopher when you might have written the truth, saying, 'I did a few Introductions and read Chrysippus' sayings, but I never entered the door of a philosopher. What share have I in the calling of Socrates, who lived and died so nobly, or of Diogenes? Can you imagine one of them weeping or indignant, because he is not going to see this man or that or be in Athens or in Corinth, but in Susa, if it so chance, or Ecbatana? Does he who may leave the banquet when he will and play no longer, vex himself while he stays on? Does he not stay at play just as long as it pleases him? Do you suppose the man I describe would endure interminable exile or condemnation to death?

Will you not be weaned at last, as children are, and take more solid food, and cease to cry 'nurse' and 'mammy', cries for old women's ears? 'But I shall distress them', you say, 'by departing.'

You will distress them? No, you will not distress them; what distresses them and you is judgement. What can you do then? Get rid of your judgement: theirs, if they do well, they will get rid of themselves, or they will sorrow for it and have themselves to thank. Man, be bold at last, even to despair, as the phrase is, that you may have peace and freedom and a lofty mind. Lift up your neck at last, as one released from slavery. Have courage to look up to God and say, 'Deal with me hereafter as Thou wilt, I am as one with Thee, I am Thine. I flinch from nothing so long as Thou thinkest it good. Lead me, where Thou wilt, put on me what raiment Thou wilt. Wouldst Thou have me hold office, or eschew it, stay or fly, be poor or rich? For all this I will defend Thee before men. I will show each thing in its true nature, as it is.'

Nay, stay rather in the cow's belly and wait for your mammy's milk to fill you. What would have become of Heracles, if he had stayed at home? He would have been Eurystheus, and no Heracles.

But tell me, how many friends and

companions had he, as he went about the world? No nearer friend than God: and that is why he was believed to be son of Zeus, and was so. Obedient to Him, he went about the world, cleansing it of wrong and lawlessness.

Do you say you are no Heracles, nor able to get rid of other men's evils, not even a Theseus, to cleanse Attica of ills?

Cleanse your own heart, cast out from your mind, not Procrustes and Sciron, but pain, fear, desire, envy, ill will, avarice, cowardice, passion uncontrolled. These things you cannot cast out, unless you look to God alone, on Him alone set your thoughts, and consecrate yourself to His commands. If you wish for anything else, with groaning and sorrow you will follow what is stronger than you, ever seeking peace outside you, and never able to be at peace: for you seek it where it is not, and refuse to seek it where it is.

CHAPTER SEVENTEEN

How we must Adjust our Primary Conceptions to Particular Things

WHAT IS THE FIRST business of the philosopher? To cast away conceit: for it is impossible for a man to begin learning what he thinks he knows. When we go to the philosophers we all bandy phrases freely of things to be done and not to be done, of things good and bad, noble and base; we make them the ground of our praise and blame, accusation and disparagement, pronouncing judgement on noble and base conduct and distinguishing between them. But what do we go to the philosophers for? To learn in their school what we think we do not know. What is that? Principles. For we want to learn what the philosophers talk of, some of us because we think their words witty and smart, and others in hope to make profit of them. It is absurd, then, to think that a man will learn anything but what he wishes to learn, or in fact that he will make progress if he does not learn. But the mass of men are under the same delusion as Theopompus the rhetor, when he criticized Plato because he wanted to define every term. What are his words?

'Did none of us before you talk of "good" or "just," or did we use the terms vaguely and idly without understanding what each of them meant?'

Who told you, Theopompus, that we had not natural notions and primary conceptions of each of these? But it is impossible to adjust the primary conceptions to the appropriate facts, without making them articulate and without considering just this–what fact must be ranged under each conception.

You may say just the same thing, for instance, to physicians. Which of us did not use the words 'healthy' and 'diseased' before Hippocrates was born? Were those terms we used mere empty sounds? No, we have a conception of 'healthy', but we cannot apply it. Therefore one physician says, 'Take no food', and another 'Give food', and one says, 'Cut the vein', and another, 'Use the cupping-glass.' What is the reason? Nothing but incapacity to apply the conception of 'the healthy' to particulars in the proper way.

So it is here in life. Which of us does not talk of 'good' and 'bad', 'expedient' and 'inexpedient'? Which of us has not a primary conception of each of these? Is that conception, then, articulate and complete? Prove it. How am I to prove it? Apply it properly to particular facts. To begin with, Plato makes his definitions conform to the conception of 'the useful', you to the conception of 'the useless'. Is it possible, then, for both of you to be right? Of course not. Does not one man apply his primary conception of 'good' to wealth while another does not? Another applies it to pleasure, another to health. To sum up, if all of us who use these terms really know them adequately as well, and if we need take no pains to make our conceptions articulate, why do we quarrel and make war and criticize one another?

Indeed, I need not bring forward our contentions with one another and make mention of them. Take yourself alone; if you apply your preconceptions properly, why do you feel miserable and hampered? Let us dismiss for the moment the Second

Department of study, that concerned with impulses and with what is fitting in relation to them. Let us dismiss also the Third Department, that of assents. I grant you all this. Let us confine' ourselves to the First Department, where we have almost sensible demonstration that we do not apply our preconceptions properly. Do you now will things possible, and possible for you? Why, then, do you feel hindered and miserable? Do you now refuse to shun what is necessary? Why, then, do you fall into trouble and misfortune? Why does a thing not happen when you will it, and happen when you do not will it, for this is the strongest proof of misery and misfortune? I will a thing, and it does not happen; what could be more wretched than I? I will it not and it happens; again, what is more wretched than I?

It was because she could not endure this that Medea was led to kill her children: and the act showed a great nature; for she had a right conception of what it means for one's will not to be realized. 'Then', said she, 'I shall thus take vengeance on him who did me wrong and outrage. Yet what is the good of putting him in this misery? What am I to do then? I kill my children, but I shall also be punishing myself. What do I care?' This is the aberration of a mind of great force; for she did not know where the power lies to do what we will; that we must not get it from outside, nor by disturbing or disarranging events. Do not will to have your husband, and then nothing that you will fails to happen. Do not will that he should live with you in all circumstances, do not will to stay in Corinth: in a word, will nothing but what God wills. Then who shall hinder you, who compel you? You will be as free as Zeus Himself.

When you have a leader such as this, and identify your will with His, you need never fear failure any more. But, once make a gift to poverty and wealth of your will to get and your will to avoid, and you will fail and be unfortunate. Give them to health and you will be unhappy: or to office, honour, country, friends, children–in a word, if you give them to anything beyond your will's control. But give them to Zeus and to the other gods; hand them to their keeping, let them control them, and command them, and you can never be miserable any more. But if, O man of no endurance, you are envious, pitiful, jealous, timorous, and never go a day without bewailing yourself and the gods, how can you call yourself a philosopher any more? Philosophy indeed! Just because you worked at variable syllogisms? Will you not unlearn all this, if you can, and begin at the beginning again, and realize that so far you never touched the matter, and, beginning here, build further on this foundation, so that nothing shall be when you will it not, nothing shall not be when you will it? Give me one young man who has come to school with this purpose, ready to strive at this, like one at the games, saying, 'For my part let all else go for nothing: I am content if I shall be allowed to spend my life unhindered and free from pain, and to lift my neck like a free man in face of facts, and to look up to heaven as God's friend, fearing nothing that can happen.' Let one of you show himself in this character, that I may say, 'Come to your own, young man: for it is your destiny to adorn philosophy, these possessions are yours, the books and theories are for you.' Then, when he has worked at this subject and made himself master of it, let him come again and say to me, 'I wish to be free from passion and disquiet, and to know in a religious and philosophic and devoted spirit how it is fitting for me to behave towards the gods, towards my parents, my brothers, my country, and towards foreigners.'

Enter now on the Second Department: this is yours too.

'Yes, but now I have studied the Second Department; next I should wish to be secure and unshaken, and that not only in my waking hours, but in my sleep and in my cups and when distraught.'

Man, you are a god, you have great designs!

'No,' he replies, 'I want to understand what Chrysippus says in his treatise on "The Liar".'

That's your design, is it, my poor fellow? Take it and go hang! What good will it do you? You will read all the treatise with sorrow and repeat it to others with trembling.

That is just how you behave. 'Would you like me to read to you, brother, and you to me?' 'Man, you are a wonderful writer': and, 'You have a great turn for Xenophon's style', and, 'You for Plato's', and, 'You for Antisthenes'.' And after all, when you have related your dreams to one another, you return again to the same behaviour as before: the same will to get and will to avoid, the same impulses and designs and purposes, the same prayers, the same interests. Then you never look for any one to remind you of the truth, but are vexed if any one reminds you. Then you say, 'He is an unamiable man; he did not weep when I left home nor say, "What difficulties you are going to! my son, if you return safe, I will light some lamps." This is what an amiable man would say.' Great good you will get if you return safe! It is worth while lighting a lamp for such as you, for you ought no doubt to be free from disease and death!

We must, then, as I say, put off this fancy of thinking that we know anything useful, and we must approach philosophy as we approach the study of geometry and music: otherwise we shall not come near making progress, even if we go through all the Introductions and treatises of Chrysippus and Antipater and Archedemus.

CHAPTER EIGHTEEN

How we must Struggle against Impressions

EVERY HABIT AND EVERY faculty is confirmed and strengthened by the corresponding acts, the faculty of walking by walking, that of running by running. If you wish to have a faculty for reading, read; if for writing, write. When you have not read for thirty days on end, but have done something else, you will know what happens. So if you lie in bed for ten days, and then get up and try to take a fairly long walk, you will see how your legs lose their power. So generally if you wish to acquire a habit for anything, do the thing; if you do not wish to acquire the habit, abstain from doing it, and acquire the habit of doing something else instead. The same holds good in things of the mind: when you are angry; know that you have not merely done ill, but that you have strengthened the habit, and, as it were, put fuel on the fire. When you yield to carnal passion you must take account not only of this one defeat, but of the fact that you have fed your incontinence and strengthened it. For habits and faculties are bound to be affected by the corresponding actions; they are either implanted if they did not exist before, or strengthened and intensified if they were there already. This is exactly how philosophers say that morbid habits spring up in the mind. For when once you conceive a desire for money, if reason is applied to make you realize the evil, the desire is checked and the Governing Principle recovers its first power; but if you give it no medicine to heal it, it will not return to where it was, but when stimulated again by the appropriate impression it kindles to desire quicker than before. And if this happens time after time it ends by growing hardened, and the weakness confirms the avarice in a man. For he who has a fever and gets quit of it is not in the same condition as before he had it, unless he has undergone a complete cure. The same sort of thing happens with affections of the mind. They leave traces behind them like weals from a blow, and if a man does not succeed in removing them, when he is flogged again on the same place his weals turn into sores. If, then, you wish not to be choleric, do not feed the angry habit, do not add fuel to the fire. To begin with, keep quiet, and count the days when you were not angry. I used to be angry every day, then every other day, then every three days, then every four. But if you miss thirty days, then sacrifice to God: for the habit is first weakened and then wholly destroyed.

I kept free from distress to-day, and again next day, and for two or three months after; and when occasions arose to provoke it, I took pains to check it.

Know that you are doing well.

To-day when I saw a handsome woman I did not say to myself, 'Would that she were mine!' and 'Blessed is her husband!' For he who says that will say, 'Blessed is the adulterer!' Nor do I picture the next scene: the woman present and disrobing and reclining by my side. I pat myself on the head and say, 'Bravo, Epictetus, you have refuted a pretty fallacy, a much prettier one than the so-called "Master"'. And if, though the woman herself, poor thing, is willing and beckons and sends to me, and even touches me and comes close to me, I still hold aloof and conquer: the refutation of this fallacy is something greater than the argument of 'The Liar', or the 'Resting' argument. This is a thing to be really proud of, rather than of propounding the 'Master' argument.

How, then, is this to be done? Make up your mind at last to please your true self, make up your mind to appear noble to God; set your desires on becoming pure in the presence of your pure self and God. 'Then when an impression of that sort assails you', says Plato [**Laws**, 854b], 'go and offer expiatory sacrifices, go as a suppliant and sacrifice to the gods who avert evil': it is enough even if 'you withdraw to the society of the good and noble' and set yourself to compare them with yourself, whether your pattern be among the living or the dead. Go to Socrates and see him reclining with Alcibiades and making light of his beauty. Consider what a victory, what an Olympic triumph, he won over himself–and knew it–what place he thus achieved among the followers of Heracles! a victory that deserves the salutation, 'Hail, admirable victor, who hast conquered something more than these worn-out boxers and pancratiasts and the gladiators who are like them!' If you set these thoughts against your impression, you will conquer it, and not be carried away by it. But first of all do not be hurried away by the suddenness of the shock, but say, 'Wait for me a little, impression. Let me see what you are, and what is at stake: let me test you'. And, further, do not allow it to go on picturing the next scene. If you do, it straightway carries you off whither it will. Cast out this filthy impression and bring in some other impression, a lovely and noble one, in its place. I say, if you acquire the habit of training yourself thus, you will see what shoulders you get, what sinews, what vigour; but now you have only paltry words and nothing more.

The man who truly trains is he who disciplines himself to face such impressions.

Stay, unhappy man! be not carried away. Great is the struggle, divine the task; the stake is a kingdom, freedom, peace, an unruffled spirit. Remember God, call Him to aid and support you, as voyagers call in storm to the Dioscuri. Can any storm be greater than that which springs from violent impressions that drive out reason? For what is storm itself but an impression? Take away the fear of death, and you may bring as much thunder and lightning as you will, and you will discover what deep peace and tranquillity is in your mind. But if you once allow yourself to be defeated and say that you will conquer hereafter, and then do the same again, be sure that you will be weak and miserable; you will never notice hereafter that you are going wrong, but will even begin to provide excuses for your conduct: and then you will confirm the truth of Hesiod's words, 'A dilatory man is ever wrestling with calamities'. [**Works and Days**, 413]

CHAPTER NINETEEN

To those who Take up the Principles of the Philosophers Only to Discuss them

THE 'MASTER' ARGUMENT APPEARS to have been propounded on some such basis as this.

There are three propositions which are at variance with one another–i.e., any two with the third–namely, these: (1) everything true as an event in the past is necessary; (2) the impossible does not follow from the possible; (3) what neither is true nor will be is yet possible. Diodorus, noticing this conflict of statements, used the probability of the first two to prove the conclusion, 'Nothing is possible which neither is nor will be true'. Some one else, however, will maintain another pair of these propositions. 'What neither is nor will be true is yet possible', and, 'The impossible does not follow from the possible', while rejecting the third, 'Everything true in the past is necessary', as appears to be the view of Cleanthes and his school, who have been supported to a large extent by Antipater. Others maintain the third pair, 'What neither is true nor will be is yet possible', and 'Everything true as an event in the past is necessary', and reject 'The impossible does not follow from the possible'. But to maintain all three propositions at once is impracticable, because every pair is in conflict with the third.

If, then, some one ask me, 'But which of these do you maintain?' I shall answer him that I do not know, but the account I have received is that Diodorus maintained one pair, and the school of Panthoides and Cleanthes, I fancy, the second, and the school of Chrysippus the third.

'What do you hold then?'

I have never given my mind to this, to put my own impression to the test and compare different views and form a judgement of my own on the subject: therefore I am no better than a grammarian.

'Who was Hector's father?'

Priam.

'Who were his brothers?'

Paris and Deiphobus.

'And who was their mother?'

Hecuba. That is the account I have received.

'From whom?'

From Homer: and Hellanicus also writes on the same subject, I believe, and others of the same class.

So it is with me and the 'Master' argument: I go no further. But if I am a vain person I cause the utmost amazement among the company at a banquet by enumerating those who have written on the subject. 'Chrysippus also has written admirably in the first book of his treatise "On the possible". Cleanthes, too, has written a special book on this, and Archedemus. And Antipater also has written, not only in his book on "The possible", but also specially in his work on "the Master" argument. Have you not read the treatise?'

'I have not read it.'

Read it.

And what good will he get from it? He will only be more silly and tiresome than he is now. For what have you got by reading it? What judgement have you formed on the subject? You will only tell us of Helen and Priam and the island of Calypso, which never was nor will be.

And indeed in the field of literature it does

not matter much that you should master the received account and have formed no judgement of your own. But we are much more liable to this fault in matters of conduct than in literary matters.

'Tell me about things good and evil.'

Listen.

From Ilion to the Cicones I came,
Wind-borne.

[Homer, **Odyssey**, IX. 39]

'Of things that are, some are good, some bad, some indifferent. The virtues and all that share in them are good, vices and all that share in them are bad, and all that comes between is indifferent–wealth, health, life, death, pleasure, pain.'

How do you know?

'Hellanicus says so in his history of Egypt.' For you might just as well say that as say 'Diogenes or Chrysippus or Cleanthes said so in his Ethics'. I ask, have you put any of these doctrines to the test, and formed a judgement of your own? Show us how you are wont to bear yourself in a storm on shipboard. Do you remember this distinction of good and bad when the sail cracks and you cry aloud to heaven, and some bystander, untimely merry, says 'Tell me, by the gods, what have you been telling us lately? Is it a vice to suffer shipwreck? Does it partake of vice?' Will you not take up a belaying pin and give him a drubbing? 'What have we to do with you, fellow? We are perishing, and you come and mock us.'

Again, if you are sent for by Caesar and are accused, do you remember the distinction? As you enter with a pale face, and trembling withal suppose some one comes up and says to you, 'Why do you tremble, man? What are you concerned about? Does Caesar put virtue and vice in the hearts of those who come before him?'

'Why do you mock me, as though I had not miseries enough?'

Nay, philosopher, tell me why you tremble. Is it not of death you stand in danger, or prison or pain of body or exile or disgrace, nothing else? Is it wickedness, or anything that partakes of wickedness? And what did you tell us that all these were?

'Man, what have Ito do with you? My own evils are enough for me.'

Well said, indeed: for your own evils are indeed enough–meanness, cowardice, the boasting spirit, which you showed when you sat in the lecture-room. Why did you pride yourself on what was not your own? Why did you call yourself a Stoic?

Watch your own conduct thus and you will discover to what school you belong. You will find that most of you are Epicureans and some few Peripatetics, but with all the fibre gone from you. Where have you shown that you really hold virtue to be equal to all else, or even superior? Show me a Stoic if you can! Where or how is he to be found? You can show me men who use the fine phrases of the Stoics, in any number, for the same men who do this can recite Epicurean phrases just as well and can repeat those of the Peripatetics just as perfectly; is it not so?

Who then is a Stoic?

Show me a man moulded to the pattern of the judgements that he utters, in the same way as we call a statue Phidian that is moulded according to the art of Phidias. Show me one who is sick and yet happy, in peril and yet happy, dying and yet happy, in exile and happy, in disgrace and happy. Show him me. By the gods I would fain see a Stoic. Nay you cannot show me a finished Stoic; then show me one in the moulding, one who has set his feet on the path. Do me this kindness, do not grudge an old man like me a sight I never saw till now. What! you think you are going to show me the Zeus of Phidias or his Athena, that work of ivory and gold? It is a soul I want; let one of you show me the soul of a man who wishes to be at one with God, and to blame God or man no longer, to fail in nothing, to feel no misfortune, to be free from anger, envy, and jealousy–one who (why wrap up my meaning?) desires to change his manhood for godhead, and who in this poor dead body of his has his purpose set upon communion with God. Show him to me. Nay, you cannot. Why, then, do you mock yourselves, and trifle with others? Why do you put on a character which is not your own, and walk about like thieves and robbers in these stolen phrases and properties that do not belong to you?

And so now I am your teacher, and you are at school with me: and my purpose is this, to make you my completed work, untouched by hindrance or compulsion, or constraint, free, tranquil, happy, looking to God in everything small or great; and you are here to learn and practise these things. Why, then, do you not finish the work, if indeed you also have the purpose you should have, and if I have the purpose and the proper equipment also? What is it that is wanting? When I see a craftsman and material ready to his hand, I look for the finished work. Now here, too, is the craftsman, and here is the material. What do we lack? Is not the subject teachable? It is teachable. Is it not within our power then? Nay, it is the one thing of all others which is in our power. Wealth is not in our power, nor health, nor anything else, in a word, except the proper use of impressions. This alone, by nature's gift, is unhindered and untrammelled. Why, then, do you not finish the work? Tell me the reason: for it lies either in me or in you or in the nature of the thing. The achievement itself is possible, and rests with us alone. It follows then that the reason lies in me or in you, or, more truly, in both. What is my conclusion? Let us begin, if you only will, to carry out such purpose here and now. Let us leave behind what is past. Only let us begin; have trust in me, and you shall see.

CHAPTER TWENTY

Against Followers of Epicurus and of the Academy

EVEN THOSE WHO CONTRADICT propositions that are true and evident are obliged to make use of them. And indeed one may almost give as the strongest proof that a thing is evident that even he who contradicts it finds himself obliged to make use of it. For instance, if one should deny that any universal statement is true, plainly he cannot help asserting the contrary.

'No universal statement is true.'

Slave, this is not true either: for what else is your assertion than, 'If a statement is universal, it is false?' Again, if one comes forward and says, 'Know that nothing is knowable, but that everything is unprovable,' or another says, 'Believe me, and it will be to your advantage; you ought not to believe a man at all'; or again, if another says, 'Learn from me, man, that it is impossible to learn anything; I tell you this, and will teach you, if you will.' What difference is there between such persons and–whom shall I say?–those who call themselves Academics? 'Men, give your assent to the statement that no man assents!'

'Believe us that no man believes any one!'

So too Epicurus, when he wishes to get rid of the natural fellowship of men with one another, makes use of the very principle of which he is getting rid. For what does he say? 'Men, be not deceived, be not misled or deluded. There is no natural fellowship of rational beings with one another: believe me. Those who state the contrary deceive you and mislead your reason.'

What concern, then, is it of yours? Let us be deceived. Will you come off any the worse if the rest of us are all convinced that we have a natural fellowship with one another and that we are bound by all means to guard it? Nay, your position will be much better and more secure. Man, why do you take thought for our sake, why do you keep awake for us, why do you light your lamp, why do you rise early, why do you write such big books? Is it to prevent any of us being deluded into thinking that the gods have any care for mankind, or to prevent us from supposing that the nature of the good is anything but pleasure? For if this is so, be off with you and go to sleep; do as the worm does, for this is the life of which you pronounce yourself worthy: eating, drinking, copulation, evacuation, and snoring.

What does it matter to you, what opinions others will hold on these matters, or whether they are right or wrong? What have we to do with you? You take interest in sheep because they offer themselves to be shorn and milked and finally to be slaughtered by us. Would it not be desirable if men could be charmed and bewitched by the Stoics into slumber, and offer themselves to you and those like you to be shorn and milked? These sentiments were proper enough to utter to your fellow Epicureans; ought you not to conceal them from outsiders, and take special pains to convince them before all things that we are born with a sociable nature, that self-control is a good thing, that so you may secure everything for yourself? Or do you say we must maintain this fellowship towards some and not towards others? Towards whom, then, must we observe it? Towards those who observe it in their turn, or towards those who transgress it? And who transgress it more completely than you who have laid down these doctrines?

What, then, was it that roused Epicurus from his slumbers and compelled him to write what he wrote? What else but that which is the most powerful of all human things, Nature, which draws a man to her will though he groan and resist? For (she says), because you hold these unsociable opinions, write them down and bequeath them to others and stay up late for them and by your own act accuse the very principles you maintain. What! we speak of Orestes pursued by the Furies and roused from his slumbers, but are not the Furies and Torments that beset Epicurus more exacting? They roused him from his sleep and would not allow him to rest, but compelled him to announce his miseries, as madness and wine compel the priests of Cybele. So powerful and unconquerable a thing is human nature. How can a vine be moved to act, not as a vine but as an olive, or again an olive not as an olive but as a vine? It is impossible, inconceivable. So it is impossible for man utterly to destroy the instincts of man; even those who have their bodily organs cut off cannot cut off the desires of men. In the same way Epicurus, though he cut off all the attributes of a man and a householder and a citizen and a friend, could not cut off human desires. No, he could not do it, any more than the indolent Academics could cast away or blind their senses, though they have made this the chief object of their life. Is not this sheer misfortune? A man has received from Nature measures and standards for the discovery of truth, and instead of busying himself to add to them and to work out further results, he does exactly the opposite, and tries to remove and destroy any faculty which he possesses for discovering the truth.

What say you, philosopher? What is your view of religion and piety?

'If you will, I will prove that it is good.'

Prove it then, that our fellow citizens may take heed and honour the Divine and cease at last from being indifferent as to the highest matters.

'Have you the proofs then?'

I have, and am thankful for it!

'Since you find such an interest in these things, now hear the contrary: "The gods do not exist, and if they do, they pay no regard to men and we have no communion with them, and thus religion and piety, of which the multitude talk, are a lie of pretentious persons and sophists, or it may be of lawgivers, for the fear and deterrence of wrongdoers."'

Bravo, philosopher! What a service you confer on our citizens! Our young men are already inclining to despise divine things, and you recover them for us!

'What is the matter? Does not this please you? Now learn, how justice is nothing, how self-respect is folly, how "father" and "son" are empty words.'

Bravo, philosopher! Stick to your task,

persuade our young men, that we may have more to agree with you and share your views. These, no doubt, are the arguments which have brought well-governed cities to greatness, these are the arguments which made Lacedaemon, these are the convictions which Lycurgus wrought into the Spartans by his laws and training: that slavery is no more shameful than noble, and freedom no more noble than shameful! For these beliefs no doubt those who died at Thermopylae died! And for what principles but these did the Athenians give up their city?

And yet the men who state these theories marry and beget children and share in city life and appoint themselves priests and prophets. Of what? Of what has no existence! And they question the Pythian prophetess themselves, to learn lies, and they interpret oracles to others. Is not this the height of shameless imposition?

Man, what are you doing? You convict

yourself of falsehood day by day: will you not abandon these crude fallacies? When you eat where do you put your hand, to your mouth or to your eye? When you bathe into what do you go? When did you ever call the jug a saucer or the ladle a spit?

If I were slave to one of these men, I would torture him, even if I had to stand a flogging from him every day. Put a drop of oil, boy, in the bath.' I would get some fish sauce and pour it over his head. 'What is that? By your fortune I had an impression, very like oil, indistinguishable from it. 'Give me gruel here.' I would fill a dish with vinegar sauce and bring it him.

'Did I not ask for gruel?'

Yes, master, this is gruel.

'Is not this vinegar sauce?'

How is it more that than gruel?

'Take it and smell, take it and taste.'

How can you know if the senses play us false? If I had three or four fellow slaves who shared my mind I should give him such a dressing that he would hang himself, or change his opinion. Such men trifle with us; they take advantage of all the gifts of nature, while in theory they do away with them.

Grateful and self-respecting men indeed! they eat bread every day, to say nothing else, and yet dare to assert that we know not whether there is a Demeter or Kore or Pluto: not to say that they enjoy day and night and the changes of the year, the stars and sea and land and the service that men render, yet not one of these things makes them take notice in the least. No, their only aim is to vomit their paltry problem, and having thus exercised their stomach to go away and have a bath. But they have not given the slightest thought to what they are going to say: what subject they are going to speak about, or to whom, and what they are going to get from these arguments: whether any young man of noble spirit may be influenced by them or has been influenced already and may lose all the germs of nobility in him: whether we may be giving an adulterer opportunity to brazen out his acts: whether one who is embezzling public funds may find some excuse to lay hold of in these theories: whether one who neglects his parents may get from them fresh courage.

What, then, do you hold good or evil, base or noble? Is it this doctrine, or that? It is useless to go on disputing with one of these men, or reasoning with him, or trying to alter his opinion. One might have very much more hope of altering the mind of a profligate than of men who are absolutely deaf and blind to their own miseries.

CHAPTER TWENTY ONE

Concerning Inconsistency of Mind

THERE ARE SOME ADMISSIONS which men readily make, others they do not. Now no one will admit that he is thoughtless or foolish: on the contrary, you will hear every one say, 'Would that I had luck as I have wits!' But men readily admit that they are cowards and say, 'I am a bit of a coward, I admit, but for the rest you will find me no fool'. A man will not readily own to incontinence, to injustice not at all, never to envy or fussiness, while most men will own to being pitiful. You ask what is the reason? The most vital reason is a confusion and want of consistency in men's views of what is good and evil, but, apart from this, different persons are affected by different motives; speaking generally, people are not ready to own to qualities which to their mind appear base. Cowardice and a sense of pity they imagine show good nature, silliness a slavish mind, and social faults they are least ready to admit. In most of the errors which they are inclined to confess to, it is because they think there is an involuntary element, as in the cowardly and the pitiful. So if any one does own to incontinence, he brings in passion, to give him the excuse of involuntary action. Injustice is in no circumstances conceived as involuntary. There is an involuntary element, they think, in jealousy, and for this reason this too is a fault which men confess.

Moving, then, as we do among men of this character, so bewildered, so ignorant of what they are saying, or of what evil is theirs, or whether they have any, or what is the reason of it, or how they are to be relieved, we ought ourselves, I think, to be constantly on our guard, asking ourselves, 'Am I too perhaps one of them? What impression have I of myself? How do I bear myself? Do I too bear myself as a man of prudence and self-control? Do I too sometimes say that I am educated to meet every emergency? Am I conscious, as the man who knows nothing should be, that I know nothing? Do I come to my teacher as to the oracles, prepared to obey, or do I too come to school like a driveller, to learn nothing but history and to understand the books which I did not understand before, and if it so chance, to expound them to others?'

Man, you have had a boxing match with your slave at home, and turned your house upside down and disturbed your neighbours, and now do you come to me with a solemn air like a wise man and sit and criticize the way I interpret language, and how I rattle out anything that comes into my head? Do you come in a spirit of envy, depressed because nothing is brought you from home, and while the discussion is going on, sit thinking of nothing yourself but how you stand with your father or your brother? 'What are men at home saying about me? They are thinking now that I am making progress and say, "He will come back knowing everything". I did indeed wish to return one day if I could, having learnt everything, but it needs hard work, and no one sends me anything and the baths are shockingly bad in Nicopolis, and I am badly off in my lodgings and in the lecture-room.'

Then they say, 'No one gets any good from the lecture-room!'

Why, who comes to the lecture-room? Who comes to be cured? Who comes to have his judgements purified? Who comes that he may grow conscious of his needs? Why are you surprised, then, that you carry away from school the very qualities you bring there, for you do not come to put away your opinions or to correct them, or to get others in exchange? No, far from it! What you must look to is whether you get what you come for. You wish to chatter about principles. Well, do you not come away with lighter tongues than before? Does not school afford you material for displaying your precious principles? Do you not analyse variable syllogisms? Do you not pursue the assumptions of 'The Liar' and hypothetical propositions? Why then do you go on being vexed at getting what you come for?

'Yes, but if my child or my brother die, or if I must be racked and die myself, what good will such things do me?'

What! is this what you came for? Is this what you sit by me for? Did you ever light your lamp or sit up late for this? Or, when you have gone out for a walk, have you ever put a conception before your mind instead of a syllogism and pursued this with your companion? When have you ever done so? Then you say, 'Principles are useless.' To whom? To those who use them wrongly. For collyrium is not useless to those who anoint themselves at the right time and in the right way, plasters are not useless, leaping-weights are not useless, but only useless to some, and again useful to others.

If you ask me now, 'Are syllogisms useful?' I shall say they are useful, and if you wish I will prove it.

'What good have they done me then?'

Man, did you ask whether they were useful in general, or useful to you? Suppose a man suffering from dysentery asked me, 'Is vinegar useful?' I shall say it is. 'Is it useful to me?' I shall say: 'No; seek first to get your flux stayed, and your ulcerations healed.' It is the same with you. You must first attend to your ulcers, and stay your flux, and arrive at peace in your mind and bring it to school undistracted, and then you will discover how wonderful the power of reason is.

CHAPTER TWENTY TWO

On Friendship

A MAN NATURALLY LOVES those things in which he is interested. Now do men take an interest in things evil? Certainly not. Do they take interest in what does not concern them? No, they do not. It follows then that they are interested in good things alone, and if interested in them, therefore love them too. Whoever then has knowledge of good things, would know how to love them; but how could one who cannot distinguish good things from evil and things indifferent from both have power to love? Therefore the wise man alone has power to love.

'Nay, how is this?' says one. 'I am not wise, yet I love my child.'

By the gods, I am surprised, to begin with, at your admission that you are not wise. What do you lack? Do you not enjoy sensation, do you not distinguish impressions, do you not supply your body with the food that is suited to it, and with shelter and a dwelling? How is it then that you admit that you are foolish? I suppose because you are often disturbed and bewildered by your impressions, and overcome by their persuasive powers, so that the very things that at one moment you consider good you presently consider bad and afterwards indifferent; and, in a word, you are subject to pain, fear, envy, confusion, change: that is why you confess yourself to be foolish. And do you not change in your affections? Do you believe at one time that wealth and pleasure and mere outward things are good, and at another time that they are evil, and do you not regard the same persons now as good, now as bad, and sometimes feel friendly towards them, sometimes unfriendly, and now praise, now blame them?

'Yes. I am subject to these feelings.'

Well then; do you think a man can be a friend to anything about which he is deceived?

'Not at all.'

Nor can he whose choice of a friend is subject to change bear good will to him?

'No, he cannot.'

Can he who first reviles a man and then admires him?

'No, he cannot.'

Again, did you never see curs fawning on one another and playing with one another, so that you say nothing could be friendlier? But to see what friendship is, throw a piece of meat among them and you will learn. So with you and your dear boy: throw a bit of land between you, and you will learn how your boy wishes to give you a speedy burial, and you pray for the boy to die. Then you cry out again, 'What a child I have reared! He is impatient to bury me'. Throw a pretty maid between you and suppose you both love her, you the old man, and he the young man. Or suppose you throw a bit of glory between you. And if you have to risk your life, you will use the words of Admetus' father:

You love the light; shall not your father love it?

[Euripides, **Alcestis**, 691]

Do you think that he did not love his own child when it was small, and was not distressed when it had the fever, and did not often say, 'Would it were I who had the fever instead!'? yet when the event came close upon him, see what words they utter! Were not Eteocles and Polynices born of the same mother and the same father? Were they not reared together, did they not live together, drink together, sleep together, often kiss one another, so that if one had seen them he would, no doubt, have laughed at the paradoxes of philosophers on friendship. Yet when the bit of meat, in the shape of a king's throne, fell between them, see what they say:

E. **Where wilt stand upon the tower?**
P. **Wherefore dost thou ask me this?**
E. **I will face thee then and slay thee**.
P. **I desire thy blood no less**.
[Euripides, **The Phoenissae**, 621]

Yes, such are the prayers they utter!

For be not deceived, every creature, to speak generally, is attached to nothing so much as to its own interest. Whatever then seems to hinder his way to this, be it a brother or a father or a child, the object of his passion or his own lover, he hates him, guards against him, curses him. For his nature is to love nothing so much as his own interest; this is his father and brother and kinsfolk and country and god. At any rate, when the gods seem to hinder us in regard to this we revile even the gods and overthrow their statues and set fire to their temples, as Alexander ordered the shrines of Asclepius to be burnt when the object of his passion died. Therefore if interest, religion and honour, country, parents and friends are set in the same scale, then all are safe; but if interest is in one scale, and in the other friends and country and kindred and justice itself, all these are weighed down by interest and disappear. For the creature must needs incline to that side where 'I' and 'mine' are; if they are in the flesh, the ruling power must be there; if in the will, it must be there; if in external things, it must be there.

If then I identify myself with my will, then and only then shall I be a friend and son and father in the true sense. For this will be my interest–to guard my character for good faith, honour, forbearance, self-control, and service of others, to maintain my relations with others. But if I separate myself from what is noble, then Epicurus' statement is confirmed, which declares that 'there is no such thing as the noble or at best it is but the creature of opinion'.

It was this ignorance that made the Athenians and Lacedaemonians quarrel with one another, and the Thebans with both, and the Great King with Hellas, and the Macedonians with Hellas and the King, and now the Romans with the Getae; and yet earlier this was the reason of the wars with Ilion. Paris was the guest of Menelaus, and any one who had seen the courtesies they used to one another would not have believed one who denied that they were friends. But a morsel was thrown between them, in the shape of a pretty woman, and for that there was war! So now, when you see friends or brothers who seem to be of one mind, do not therefore pronounce upon their friendship, though they swear to it and say it is impossible for them to part with one another. The Governing Principle of the bad man is not to be trusted; it is uncertain, irresolute, conquered now by one impression, now by another. The question you must ask is, not what others ask, whether they were born of the same parents and brought up together and under the charge of the same slave; but this question only, where they put their interest–outside them or in the will. If they put it outside, do not call them friends, any more than you can call them faithful, or stable, or confident, or free; nay, do not call them even men, if you are wise. For it is no human judgement which makes them bite one another and revile one another and occupy deserts or market-places like wild beasts and behave like robbers in the law-courts; and which makes them guilty of profligacy and adultery and seduction and the other offences men commit against one another. There is one judgement and one only which is responsible for all this–that they set themselves and all their interests elsewhere than in their will. But if you hear that these men in very truth believe the good to lie only in the region of the will and in dealing rightly with impressions, you need trouble yourself no more as to whether a man is son or father, whether they are brothers, or have been familiar companions for years; I say, if you grasp this one fact and no more, you may pronounce with confidence that they are friends, as you may that they are faithful and just. For where else is friendship but where faith and honour are, where men give and take what is good, and nothing else?

'But he has paid me attention all this time: did he not love me?'

How do you know, slave, whether he has paid you this attention, as a man cleans his boots, or tends his beast? How do you know whether, when you have lost your use as a paltry vessel, he will not throw you away like a broken plate?

'But she is my wife and we have lived together this long time.'

How long did Eriphyle live with Amphiaraus, ay, and was mother of many children?–But a necklace came between them.

'What do you mean by a necklace?'

Man's judgement about good and evil. This was the brutish element, this was what broke up the friendship, which suffered not the wife to be true to her wedlock, nor the mother to be a mother indeed. So let every one of you, who is anxious himself to be friend to another, or to win another for his friend, uproot these judgements, hate them, drive them out of his mind. If he does that, then first he will never revile himself or be in conflict with himself, he will be free from change of mind, and self-torture; secondly he will be friendly to his neighbour, always and absolutely, if he be like himself, and if he be unlike, he will bear with him, be gentle and tender with him, considerate to him as one who is ignorant and in error about the highest matters; not hard upon any man, for he knows of a certainty Plato's saying, 'No soul is robbed of the truth save involuntarily'.

But if you fail to do this, you may do everything else that friends do –drink together and live under the same roof and sail in the same ship and be born of the same parents; well, the same may be true of snakes, but neither they nor you will be capable of friendship so long as you retain these brutish and revolting judgements.

CHAPTER TWENTY THREE

On the Faculty of Expression

EVERY ONE CAN READ a book with the more pleasure and ease the plainer the letters in which it is written. So too every one can listen more easily to discourse which is expressed in becoming and distinguished language. We must therefore not say that the faculty of expression is nothing. To say so is at once irreligious and cowardly; irreligious because it means disparaging

God's gifts, just as though one should deny the usefulness of the faculty of vision or hearing or even the faculty of speech. Was it for nothing then that God gave you your eyes? Was it for nothing He mingled with them a spirit so powerful and cunningly devised, that even from a distance they can fashion the shapes of what they see? And what messenger is so swift and attentive as they? Was it for nothing that He made the intervening air so active and sensitive that vision passes through it as through a tense medium? Was it for nothing that He made light, without the presence of which all the rest would have been useless?

Man, be not ungrateful, nor again forget higher things! Give thanks to God for sight and hearing, yes, and for life itself and what is conducive to life–for grain and fruit, for wine and oil; but remember that He has given you another gift superior to all these, the faculty which shall use them, test them, and calculate the value of each. For what is it that pronounces on each of these faculties, and decides their value? Is it the faculty itself, in each case? Did you ever hear the faculty of vision saying anything about itself, or the faculty of hearing? No, these faculties are ordained as ministers and slaves to serve the faculty which deals with impressions. And if you ask what each is worth, whom do you ask? Who answers you? How then can any other faculty be superior to this, which uses the rest as its servants and itself tests each result and pronounces on it? Which of those faculties knows what it is and what it is worth, which of them knows when it ought to be used and when it ought not? What is the faculty that opens and closes the eyes and brings them near some objects and turns them away, at need, from others? Is it the faculty of vision? No, it is the faculty of will. What is it that closes and opens the ears? What is it that makes us curious and questioning, or again unmoved by discourse? Is it the faculty of hearing? It is no other faculty but that of the will.

I say, when the will sees that all the other faculties which surround it are blind and deaf and are unable to see anything else beyond the very objects for which they are ordained to minister to this faculty and serve it, and this alone has clear sight and surveys the rest and itself and estimates their value, is it likely to pronounce that any other faculty but itself is the highest? What is the function of the eye, when opened, but to see? But what is it tells us whether we ought to look at a man's wife or how? The faculty of will. What tells us whether we ought to believe or disbelieve what we are told, and if we believe whether we are to be excited or not? Is it not the faculty of will? This faculty of eloquence I spoke of, if such special faculty there be, concerned with the framing of fair phrases, does no more than construct and adorn phrases, when there is an occasion for discourse, just as hairdressers arrange and adorn the hair. But whether it is better to speak or be silent, and to speak in this way or that, and whether it is proper or improper–in a word, to decide the occasion and the use for each discourse, all these are questions for one faculty only, that of the will. Would you have it come forward and pronounce against itself?

'But', says the objector, 'what if the matter stands thus, what if that which ministers can be superior to that which it serves, the horse to the horseman, the hound to the hunter, the lyre to him that plays it, the servants to the king they serve?' The answer is: What is it that uses other things? The will. What is it that attends to everything? The will. What is it that destroys the whole man, now by starvation, now by a halter, now by a headlong fall? The will. Is there then anything stronger in men than this? Nay, how can things that are subject to hindrance be stronger than that which is unhindered? What has power to hinder the faculty of vision? Will and events beyond the will. The faculty of hearing and that of speech are subject to the same hindrance. But what can hinder the will? Nothing beyond the will, only the perversion of the will itself. Therefore vice or virtue resides in this alone. Yet being so mighty a faculty, ordained to rule all the rest, you would have it come forward and tell us that the flesh is of all things most excellent. Why, if the flesh itself asserted that it was the most excellent of things, one would not tolerate it even then. But as it is, Epicurus, what is the faculty that pronounces this judgement? Is it the faculty which has written on 'The End' or 'Physics' or 'The Standard'? The faculty which made you grow your beard as a philosopher? which wrote in the hour of death 'I am living my last day and that a blessed one'? Is this faculty flesh or will? Surely it is madness to admit that you have a faculty superior to this. Can you be in truth so blind and deaf?

What follows? Do we disparage the other

faculties? God forbid. Do we say that there is no use nor advancement save in the faculty of will? God forbid! That were foolish, irreligious, ungrateful toward God. We are only giving each thing its due. For there is use in an ass, but not so much as in an ox; there is use in a dog, but not so much as in a servant; there is use in a servant, but not so much as in a fellow-citizen; there is use in them too, but not so much as in those who govern them. Yet because other faculties are higher we must not depreciate the use which inferior faculties yield. The faculty of eloquence has its value, but it is not so great as that of the will; but when I say this, let no one suppose that I bid you neglect your manner of speech, any more than I would have you neglect eyes or ears or hands or feet or clothes or shoes.

But if you ask me, 'What then is the highest of all things,' what am I to say? The faculty of speech? I cannot say that. No, the faculty of will, when it is in the right way. For it is this which controls the faculty of speech and all other faculties small and great. When this is set in the right course, a man becomes good; when it fails, man becomes bad; it is this which makes our fortune bad or good, this which makes us critical of one another or well content; in a word, to ignore this means misery, to attend to it means happiness.

Yet to do away with the faculty of eloquence and deny its existence is indeed not only ungrateful to those who have given it, but shows a coward's spirit. For he who denies it seems to me to fear that, if there is a faculty of eloquence, we may not be able to despise it. It is just the same with those who deny that there is any difference between beauty and ugliness. What! are we to believe that the sight of Thersites could move men as much as the sight of Achilles, and the sight of Helen no more than the sight of an ordinary woman? No, these are the words of foolish and uneducated persons, who do not know one thing from another, and who fear that if once one becomes aware of such differences, one may be overwhelmed and defeated.

No, the great thing is this–to leave each in possession of his own faculty, and so leaving him to see the value of the faculty, and to understand what is the highest of all things and to pursue this always, and concentrate your interest on this, counting all other things subordinate to this, yet not failing to attend to them too so far as you may. For even to the eyes you must attend, yet not as though they were the highest, but to these also for the sake of the highest; for the highest will not fulfil its proper nature unless it uses the eyes with reason, and chooses one thing rather than another.

What then do we see men doing? They are like a man returning to his own country who, finding a good inn on his road, stays on there because it pleases him. Man, you are forgetting your purpose! You were not travelling to this, but through it.

'Yes, but this is a fine inn.'

And how many other fine inns are there, and how many fine meadows? But they are merely to pass through; your purpose is yonder; to return to your country, to relieve your kinsfolk of their fears, to fulfil your own duties as a citizen, to marry, beget children, and hold office in due course. For you have not come into the world to choose your pick of fine places, but to live and move in the place where you were born and appointed to be a citizen. The same principle holds good in what we are discussing. Our road to perfection must needs lie through instruction and the spoken word; and one must purify the will and bring into right order the faculty which deals with impressions; and principles must be communicated in a particular style, with some variety and epigram. But this being so, some people are attracted by the very means they are using and stay where they are, one caught by style, another by syllogisms, a third by variable arguments, and a fourth by some other seductive inn by the way; and there they stay on and moulder away, like those whom the Sirens entertain.

Man, the purpose set before you was to make yourself capable of dealing with the impressions that you meet as nature orders, so as not to fail in what you will to get, nor to fall into what you will to avoid, never suffering misfortune or bad fortune, free, unhindered, unconstrained, conforming to the governance of God, obeying this, well pleased with this, criticizing none, blaming none, able to say these lines with your whole heart,

Lead me, O Zeus, and thou my Destiny.
[Cleanthes]

Having this purpose before you, are you going to stay where you are just because a pretty phrase or certain precepts please you, and choose to make your home there, forgetting what you have left at home, and say, ‘These things are fine’? Who says they are not fine? But they are fine as things to pass through, as inns by the way. What prevents you from being unfortunate, though you speak like Demosthenes? Though you can analyse syllogisms like Chrysippus, what prevents you from being wretched, mournful, envious–in a word, bewildered and miserable? Nothing prevents you. Do you see then that these were inns of no value; and the goal set before you was different? Certain persons when I say this think I am disparaging the study of rhetoric or of principles. No, I am not depreciating that, but only the tendency to dwell unceasingly on such matters and to set your hopes on them. If any man does his hearers harm by bringing this truth home to them, count me among those who do this harm. But when I see that what is highest and most sovereign is something different, I cannot say that it is what it is not in order to gratify you.

CHAPTER TWENTY FOUR

To One whom he did not Think Worthy

SOME ONE SAID TO him, ‘I often came to you, desiring to hear you and you never gave me an answer, and now, if it may be, I beg you to say something to me’.

Do you think, he replied, that there is an art of speaking, like other arts, and that he who has it will speak with skill and he who has it not, without skill?

'I think so.'

Is it true then that he who by his speech gains benefit himself and is able to benefit others would speak with skill, and he who tends to be harmed himself and harm others would be unskilled in the art of speaking?

'Yes, you would find that some are harmed, some benefited.'

But what of the hearers? Are they all benefited by what they hear, or would you find that of them too some are benefited and some harmed?

'Yes, that is true of them too', he said.

Here too then it is true that those who hear with skill are benefited, and those who hear without skill are harmed?

He agreed.

Is there then a skill in hearing as well as in speaking?

'So it appears.'

If you will, look at the question thus. Whose part do you think it is to touch an instrument musically?

'The musician's.'

And whose part do you think it is to make a statue properly?

'The sculptor's.'

Does it not seem to you to require any art to look at a statue with skill?

'Yes, this requires art too.'

If then right speaking demands a skilled person, do you see that hearing with profit also demands a skilled person? As for perfection and profit in the full sense, that, if you like, we may for the moment dismiss, as we are both far from anything of that sort; but this I think every one would admit, that he who is to listen to philosophers must have at least some practice in listening. Is it not so?

Show me then what it is you would have me speak to you about. What are you able to hear about? About things good and bad? Good what? A good horse?

'No.'

A good ox?

'No.'

What then? A good man?

'Yes.'

Do we know then what man is, what his nature is, what the notion is? Are our ears open in any degree with regard to this? Nay, do you understand what Nature is, or can you in any measure follow me when I speak? Am I to demonstrate to you? How am I to do it? Do you really understand what demonstration is, or how a thing is demonstrated, or by what means, or what processes are like demonstration without being demonstrations? Do you know what is true or what is false, what follows what, what is in conflict, or disagreement or discord with what? Can I rouse you to philosophy? How can I show you the conflict of the multitude, their disputes as to things good and evil, useful and harmful, when you do not so much as know what conflict is? Show me then what good I shall do you by conversing with you.

'Rouse my interest.'

As the sheep when he sees the grass that suits him has his desire roused to eat, but if you set a stone or loaf by him he will not be roused, so there are in us certain natural inclinations toward discourse, when the appropriate hearer appears and provokes the inclination; but if he lies there like a stone or a piece of grass, how can he rouse a man's will? Does the vine say to the farmer, 'Attend to me'? No, its very appearance shows that it will be to his profit to attend to it and so calls out his energies. Who does not answer the call of winning and saucy children to play with them and crawl with them and talk nonsense with them, but who wants to play or bray with an ass? However small he may be, he is still an ass.

'Why then do you say nothing to me?'

There is only one thing I can say to you, that he who is ignorant who he is and for what he is born and what the world is that he is in and who are his fellows, and what things are good and evil, noble and base; who cannot understand reasoning or demonstration, or what is true or what false, and is unable to distinguish them, such a man will not follow nature in his will to get or to avoid, in his impulses or designs, in assent, refusal, or withholding of assent; to sum up, he will go about the world deaf and blind, thinking himself somebody, when he is really nobody. Do you think there is anything new in this? Ever since the race of men began, have not all errors and misfortunes arisen from this ignorance?

Why did Agamemnon and Achilles quarrel with one another? Was it not because they did not know what was expedient or inexpedient? Did not one say that it was expedient to give back Chryseis to her father, and the other that it was not? Did not one say that he ought to take the other's prize, and the other that he ought not? Did not this too make them forget who they were and for what they had come?

Let be, man, what have you come for? To win women for your love or to make war?

'To make war.'

With whom? Trojans or Greeks?

'Trojans.'

Why then do you leave Hector and draw your sword on your own king? And you, best of men, have you left your duties as a king,

trusted with clans and all their mighty cares,

[Homer, **Iliad**, II. 25]

to fight a duel for a paltry damsel with the most warlike of your allies, whom you ought by all means to respect and guard? Do you show yourself inferior to the courteous high priest who pays all attention to you noble gladiators? Do you see what ignorance as to things expedient leads to?

'But I too am rich.'

Are you any richer than Agamemnon?

'But I am handsome as well.'

Are you any handsomer than Achilles?

'But I have a fine head of hair.'

Had not Achilles a finer, and golden hair too, and he did not comb and smooth it to look fine?

'But I am strong.'

Can you lift a stone as big as Hector or Ajax could?

'But I am noble too.'

Was your mother a goddess, or your father of the seed of Zeus? What good do these things do Achilles, when he sits weeping for his darling mistress?

'But I am an orator.'

And was not he? Do not you see how he handled Odysseus and

Phoenix, the most eloquent of the Hellenes, how he shut their mouths? This is all I can say to you, and even this I have no heart for. 'Why?'

Because you do not excite my interest. Is there anything in you to excite me as men who keep horses are excited at sight of a well-bred horse? Your poor body? You make an ugly figure. Your clothes? They are too luxurious. Your air, your countenance? There is nothing to see. When you wish to hear a philosopher, do not say to him, 'You say nothing to me,' but only show yourself worthy to hear and you will see how you will rouse him to discourse!

CHAPTER TWENTY FIVE

How the Art of Reasoning is Necessary

WHEN ONE OF HIS audience said, 'Convince me that logic is useful,' he said,

Would you have me demonstrate it?

'Yes.'

Well, then, must I not use a demonstrative argument?

And, when the other agreed, he said, How

then shall you know if I impose upon you? And when the man had no answer, he said, You see how you yourself admit that logic is necessary, if without it you are not even able to learn this much–whether it is necessary or not.

CHAPTER TWENTY SIX

What is the Distinctive Character of Error

EVERY ERROR IMPLIES CONFLICT; for since he who errs does not wish to go wrong but to go right, plainly he is not doing what he wishes. For what does the thief wish to do? What is to his interest. If then thieving is against his interest, he is not doing what he wishes. But every rational soul by nature dislikes conflict; and so, as long as a man does not understand that he is in conflict, there is nothing to prevent him from doing conflicting acts, but, whenever he understands, strong necessity makes him abandon the conflict and avoid it, just as bitter necessity makes a man renounce a falsehood when he discovers it, though as long as he has not this impression he assents to it as true.

He then who can show to each man the conflict which causes his error, and can clearly bring home to him how he fails to do what he wishes and does what he does not wish, is powerful in argument and strong to encourage and convict. For if one shows this, a man will retire from his error of himself; but as long as you do not succeed in showing this, you need not wonder if he persists in his error, for he acts because he has an impression that he is right. That is why Socrates too, relying on this faculty, said, 'I am not wont to produce any other witness to support what I say, but am content with him to whom I am talking on each occasion; it is his vote that I take, his evidence that I call, and his sole word suffices instead of all.' For Socrates knew what moves the rational soul, and that it will incline to what moves it, whether it wishes to or not. Show the conflict to the rational Governing Principle and it will desist. If you do not show it, blame yourself rather than him who refuses to obey.

CONTINUES IN VOLUME TWO

www.ingramcontent.com/pod-product-compliance
Lightning Source LLC
Chambersburg PA
CBHW020915310726
48980CB00011B/904/J

* 9 7 8 1 8 3 4 1 2 3 8 9 9 *